SEMEIA 24

Old Testament Interpretation from a Process Perspective

Editors of This Issue:
William A. Beardslee
David J. Lull

© 1982
by the Society of Biblical Literature

Published by
SCHOLARS PRESS
101 Salem Street
P.O. Box 2268
Chico, CA 95927

Manufactured in the U.S.A.

CONTENTS

Contributors to This Issue iv

ARTICLES AND RESPONSES

Introduction
   William A. Beardslee and David J. Lull 1

Metaphor and Reality in Hosea 11
   J. Gerald Janzen 7

Response to Janzen: "Metaphor and Reality in Hosea 11"
   James Luther Mays 45

The Way of Obedience: Traditio-Historical
and Hermeneutical Reflections on the Balaam Story
   George W. Coats 53

The Divine Curse Understood in Terms of Persuasion
   Lewis S. Ford 81

Trajectories and Historic Routes
   John B. Cobb, Jr. 89

Cobb's Living Historic Routes: A Response
   Kent Harold Richards 99

Process Hermeneutic: Promise and Problems
   John J. Collins 107

CONTRIBUTORS TO THIS ISSUE

William A. Beardslee
　　Department of Religion
　　Emory University
　　Atlanta, GA 30322

George W. Coats
　　Lexington Theological Seminary
　　631 South Limestone Street
　　Lexington, KY 40508

John B. Cobb, Jr.
　　School of Theology at Claremont
　　1325 North College Avenue
　　Claremont, CA 91711

John J. Collins
　　Department of Religious Studies
　　DePaul University
　　2323 North Seminary Avenue
　　Chicago, IL 60614

Lewis S. Ford
　　Department of Philosophy
　　Old Dominion University
　　Norfolk, VA 23508

J. Gerald Janzen
　　Christian Theological Seminary
　　1000 West 42nd Street
　　Indianapolis, IN 46208

David J. Lull
　　Yale Divinity School
　　409 Prospect Street
　　New Haven, CT 06510

James Luther Mays
　　Union Theological Seminary in Virginia
　　3401 Brook Road
　　Richmond, VA 23227

Kent Harold Richards
　　Iliff School of Theology
　　2201 South University Boulevard
　　Denver, CO 80210

ACKNOWLEDGMENTS

METAPHOR AND REALITY IN HOSEA 11 by J. Gerald Janzen
    Revised version of an essay of the same title published in *SBL Seminar Papers, 1976* (Missoula: Scholars, 1976), pp. 412–45.

RESPONSE TO JANZEN: "METAPHOR AND REALITY IN HOSEA 11" by James Luther Mays
    Previously unpublished response to Janzen presented at the 1976 SBL Process Hermeneutic and Biblical Exegesis Group, SBL Annual Meeting.

THE WAY OF OBEDIENCE by George W. Coats
    This essay represents an expanded and completely revised version of "Baalam: Sinner or Saint," *BR* 18 (1973) 21–29.

TRAJECTORIES AND HISTORIC ROUTES by John B. Cobb, Jr.
    Previously unpublished paper presented to the SBL Process Hermeneutic and Biblical Exegesis Group, SBL Annual Meeting, 1975.

INTRODUCTION

William A. Beardslee
Emory University
and
David J. Lull
Yale Divinity School

ABSTRACT

The following collection of essays represents an advanced stage of the discussion of the fruitfulness of an interaction between Old Testament studies and process thought. Two of the essays, and their responses, further develop the interpretation of divine power as persuasive and of God's actuality as contingent by directing attention to the formal traits of particular texts. This collection also includes an essay and response in which the emphasis is on the nature of tradition, which regards the reader as a participant in a creative process, and places in question the effort to define a tradition in terms of an essence or fixed, enduring quality.

1.1   A theory of interpretation may center upon one or more of several factors in the interpretive process: the world of reality with which the text deals, the author, the form of the text or the nature of language, and the reader of the text would be classical examples (see Gunn, following Abrams: 3-29). Most Old Testament interpretation from a process perspective has concentrated upon the first of these possible centers and has dealt primarily with a reconceptualizing of the transcendent God of the Old Testament in the direction of the process God of persuasion/1/. It is easy to understand why this course has been followed, since the process vision of God as a God of persuasion, a God who is not in total control but who gently and patiently leads or lures events toward their final forms of actuality, was originally developed by A. N. Whitehead (at least in part) in conscious reaction against what he perceived to be the tyrannical, monarchical God of the Old Testament (1969:54-55; 1978:342-43). A process reading of the Hebrew Scriptures thus has been a challenge to bring into the center of attention elements in those Scriptures which offer images of divine persuasion, so that both general readers and those in religious communities who read these books as Scripture may find in them a legitimizing base for such a vision of God; but process reading has also been a call for the rejection of those metaphors and stories in the Hebrew Scriptures which inescapably carry the message of inevitable divine determination.

1.2   The present collection carries this discussion forward in two focal essays and the comments on them: the essays by J. Gerald Janzen (with comment by James Luther Mays) and by George W. Coats (with comment by Lewis S. Ford). In both cases the theological issues are set in close relation to formal analyses of the texts.

2.1   Coats frames his theological reflection in a close form- and tradition-historical study of the complex Balaam tradition. He discerns two genres which have been fused in the existing text: a legend, in which Balaam is a "saint," a model of complete prophetic obedience, and a fable, in which Balaam is resistant to the divine will which triumphs in spite of human rebellion. It is clear to Coats that the obedient prophet legend and indeed the whole type which it represents are highly amenable to interpretation in terms of divine persuasion, but that the fable of God's overcoming human resistance in spite of all is not. His reflections carry him into the question of the canon as Scripture for a changing community, which relates his work to that of John B. Cobb, Jr. (see below, §§4.1–4.4). In particular, Coats sees that the relatively stable generic forms (in this case, legend) provide one of the elements of stability in the flux of "historic routes of living occasions" that Cobb sketches—a theme that requires further exploration.

2.2   But Coats's principal move toward enriching process reflection on the Hebrew Scriptures is his study of the stubborn theme of the divine curse, so resistant to interpretation in much modern theology. Coats rightly sees the highly social and historical context of the image of the divine curse, which deals with consequences of earlier actions. It is at this point that his reflections are taken up by Ford, who asks what the divine curse could mean in a process perspective, and who provides a possible answer from a modified Whiteheadian perspective. Whether or not modern readers will find the image of the divine curse an acceptable one, this discussion, if cast in terms of divine discipline, points to an area that cannot be neglected without threatening the breakdown of faith in the connection between God and the successive moments of experience.

3.1   Janzen's paper is like Coats's in setting the process reflections in the context of a close attention to the form of the texts. His study of Hosea 11 embodies a rich lexical and grammatical analysis of the crucial verse 11:8b, which opens the way for reflection about the divine act of decision on the analogy of the human act of "existential decision," in which the self is open to reconstitution in a new direction. Janzen's work raises the question of the scope of analogy in speaking of God and serves as a reminder that language about God is a central part of process theology, in contrast to so much contemporary theology and hermeneutic, which limit themselves to the human situation and the response of faith.

3.2   Mays in his comment shows great appreciation for Janzen's close analysis of the texts, and modifies his previous translation of Hos 11:8b in the light of Janzen's work. He also appreciates Janzen's emphasis on the dynamic aspect of God's existence; but he sees the metaphor of existential decision as implying that there are no determinate elements in God's decision. He finds Karl Barth's way of speaking of the interplay between the immutable and the mutable aspects of the divine existence more appropriate to the text. The discussion should open the way for further exploration of this important topic.

4.1   While Coats and Janzen have worked with the world of the text, and have amplified the previous study of this topic from a process point of view by their close attention to the form of the text, Cobb applies a process conceptuality primarily to interaction between the reader and the text. The contribution of process thought to the discussion about the nature and function of texts and language is thus approached from two directions in these essays but not explored frontally in any of them/2/.

4.2   Cobb does not deal directly at all with the principal theological problem of the previous discussion; the term God does not even appear in his essay. The process view of God is implied, however, in his remarks about the vitality of orientation toward the future and the encouragement of novel forms.

4.3   Neither does Cobb turn his attention to the nature of texts and their internal relations, a subject which is so important in many contemporary theories of interpretation. What interests him is the process of the transmission of tradition as a creative process, understood in terms of a philosophy of events, in which the meanings of texts (and other carriers of tradition) are understood as internally related both to their originating events and to the events along the path of their transmission. Taking up James M. Robinson's term "trajectory," he modifies the intention of Robinson to give the developing course of events in a community a more living character than is suggested either by the term tradition or by trajectory. While most inquiries into the nature of the connection between the past and the present have sought for ways of establishing some unchanged term, an essence or stable quality, in the connection between the classic originating events and later times, Cobb looks instead for something in the form of the change to provide a test of authentic connection with the past.

4.4   His work reopens the question of how to understand the impetus for change in Hebrew and Jewish faith and in Jesus and early Christianity. It is at this point that his work, with illustrations drawn principally from the

New Testament, connects with the other essays and with the theme of the God of persuasion.

4.5   In his comment, Kent H. Richards notes that, although the present phase of the hermeneutical discussion focuses on literature and language rather than on history, Cobb's concept of a "living historic route" does contribute to the current interest in the indeterminacy of meaning. It challenges both the distancing of the biblical scholar from the text and the location of normativity only within the text, which are implicit in traditional methods of historical and literary criticism. And it suggests an interpretive task that does not end with mere description and suspended judgment but is essentially an imaginative act that includes inheritance, synthesis and modification. From this perspective, Richards suggests, a process interpretation of Lev 27:1-8, for example, would take account of the formative events out of which the text itself evolved as well as those of successive interpretations of the seasons of life within Judaism and early Christianity and on up to the present. The result is an interpretation that is faithful to the text's intention to dedicate persons to the sanctuary without the necessity of conforming to the text's forms of sexist and ageist valuations of persons. In such a way interpretation can be faithful to the text without being slavishly bound to it.

5.1   Collins's discussion of the promise and problems of process hermeneutic probes that perspective particularly at two points: the process view of God, and the normative nature of the biblical text for theological understanding. Collins rightly sees that a whole way of thinking is involved. It is a way of thinking in which only the actual can act; and that is why in process thought God is an actual entity related to but not identified with "nature," which is not an actual entity but an aggregate of many actual entities. This presupposition, that only the actual can act, stands in marked contrast to the whole phenomenological tradition with its "bracketing," which has been so influential in contemporary theories of interpretation.

5.2   Similarly, it is Cobb's effort to develop an account of historical change which is indeed, as Collins desires, a socio-historical approach, yet not a reductionist one, that leads him to adopt the process modification of the image of "trajectory." Though there is a great variety among process theologians, most of them recognize the ideological element in the Scriptures quite directly. But most of them would probably also wish to balance an explanation of tradition in terms of socio-historical factors with a recognition that persons and communities of religious faith really know something about the reality with which they deal. Such persons uniformly ascribe a referential quality to their assertions about the object of their faith which not only deals with human emotions and socio-historical factors as such, but also sees these as expressions of interaction with and response to a larger whole and "eros" (or lure)—indeed, to God. To assess such assertion critically and publicly is no easy task, and those of us who work with process categories are indebted to Collins for probing our perspective as he has.

5.3   It can also be hoped that the process approach may further clarify the nature of the public discourse which Collins calls for. Recognizing the validity of confessional approaches within their own sphere, most process thinkers also recognize the perspectival element in every position, but do not believe that such a recognition must lead to a reductive or merely relativist conclusion (Cobb:252–84, esp. 267–68).

6.1   Richards remarks in his response to Cobb that the contribution which process thought might make to an understanding of language and texts is not developed in Cobb's article, which deals rather with problems of history. Reflecting on the collection as a whole, one may hope that a process realism, open to the referential dimension of metaphor and analogy yet critical of any naive correspondence view, may become more articulate at this point, which lies between the world of the text on the one hand, explored by Coats and Janzen, and the reader's world, situated in a historical route of living occasions explored by Cobb. The very fact that so many theories of imagination and language, and hence many types of literary criticism, pay little attention to the dimension of reference (see Detweiler), makes the potential of a process contribution the more important.

NOTES

/1/   For the previous process discussion of divine power in the OT, see Coats (1977), Ford (1971 and 1978:15–44), Griffin, and Janzen (1975).

/2/   For a discussion of the nature and function of texts and language from a process perspective, see Beardslee and Lull (eds.) and the bibliography cited there (1979:27–30 and 31–37).

WORKS CONSULTED

Abrams, M. H.
    1953   *The Mirror and the Lamp: Romantic Theory and Critical Tradition.* London: Oxford University.

Beardslee, William A. and Lull, David J. (eds.)
    1979   Thematic Issue: "New Testament Interpretation from a Process Perspective." *JAAR* 47:21–128.

Coats, George W.
    1977   "The King's Loyal Opposition: Obedience and Authority in Exodus 32–34." Pp. 91–109 in *Canon and Authority: Essays in Old Testament Religion and Theology*. Eds. G. W. Coats and B. O. Long. Philadelphia: Fortress.

Cobb, John B., Jr.
    1965   *A Christian Natural Theology: Based on the Thought of Alfred North Whitehead*. Philadelphia: Westminster.

Detweiler, Robert
    1980   "After the New Criticism: Contemporary Methods of Literary Interpretation." Pp. 5–23 in *Orientation by Disorientation: Studies in Literary Criticism and Biblical Literary Criticism Presented in Honor of William A. Beardslee*. Ed. R. A. Spencer. PTMS 35. Pittsburgh: Pickwick.

Ford, Lewis S.
    1971   "God as King: Benevolent Despot or Constitutional Monarch?" *Christian Scholar's Review* 1:318–22.

    1978   *The Lure of God: A Biblical Background for Process Theism*. Philadelphia: Fortress.

Griffin, David R.
    1975   "Relativism, Divine Causation, and Biblical Theology." *Encounter* 36:342–60.

Gunn, Giles B.
    1971   "Introduction: Literature in Its Relation to Religion." Pp. 1–33 in *Literature and Religion*. Ed. G. B. Gunn. New York: Harper and Row.

Janzen, J. Gerald
    1975   "Modes of Power and the Divine Relativity." *Encounter* 36:379–406.

Whitehead, Alfred North
    1969   *Religion in the Making*. Cleveland/New York: Meridian/World. Original, 1926.

    1978   *Process and Reality: An Essay in Cosmology*. Corrected Edition. Eds. D. R. Griffin and D. W. Sherburne. New York: Free Press/Macmillan. Original, 1929.

METAPHOR AND REALITY IN HOSEA 11

J. Gerald Janzen
Christian Theological Seminary

ABSTRACT

Among the various modes of divine address to Israel found in Hosea is that mode which takes the form of a question. It is the purpose of this paper to explore the theological implications of this mode of address in Hosea, especially in the climactic instance in Chapter 11. This exploration is based on a consideration of what it means to ask oneself a question, what it means to ask the same question of another, and what it might mean for God to ask questions of self and of others. It is proposed that such an approach enables a fresh angle of vision on the biblical portrayals of covenant as a temporal dynamic. It is proposed also that the questioning mode of address in Hosea 11 confronts the impasse in the covenant relation in such a way as to indicate the gravity of the factors making for the impasse and yet (in virtue of its questioning mode) to intimate the possibility of an open future for the covenant relation, a future which imparts eschatological character both to human life and, it may be, to the life of God.

0.1   Among the various modes of divine address to Israel which are to be found in the Book of Hosea is that mode which takes the grammatical form of a question. This mode of address occurs only sparingly, yet it punctuates the divine address as a whole in such a way as to imbue the whole with its own peculiar significance. This is especially the case in chapter 11, where a divine question to the people inaugurates perhaps the boldest portrayal of "the living God" in the Old Testament. It is the purpose of this paper to explore the theological implications of this mode of address in Hosea, especially in its climactic occurrence in chapter 11. This exploration will involve a consideration of what it means to ask oneself a question, what it means to ask that question of another, and what it might mean for God to ask questions of self and of others.

0.2   Given the character of the exploration undertaken in this paper, I should say something at the outset about hermeneutical method. I characteristically try to approach a text with no specific posture or strategy, but with a sort of general alert emptiness—what Alan Watts, I suppose, might call

Kendo—in which the sum total of what I know about things sleeps in readiness within me/1/. The general intention is to allow the text to set the agenda by raising questions or posing issues or opening perspectives through the specific elements of the text which claim my special interest. When such interest has been awakened, I pursue it in whatever fashion, or with whatever combination of resources of understanding, seems to offer promise of illuminating the text. The control on such a pursuit is, of course, the text itself. In my view, the pursuit may operate on as short or as long a leash as one's hermeneutical imagination is comfortable with, so long as, in the end, the results respect the integrity, and indeed illuminate the integrity, of the text. In the terms employed in the present paper, the question of hermeneutical method at bottom is an *existential* question, and as such can be answered only at the *end* of the hermeneutical process.

0.3   Since this paper is quite long, I shall outline the course which my exploration of Hosea 11 will take. *First*, I will place the topic before us by a simple presentation of the relevant texts, together with a brief comment on their contexts, and with some quotations from the commentaries of James Luther Mays and Hans Walter Wolff which will provide a point of entry into my hermeneutical explorations. *Secondly*, I will engage in some general reflection on what it means to ask a question, for us, and possibly for God. *Thirdly*, I will consider briefly several aspects of the Old Testament from the perspective gained through the general reflection. *Fourthly*, I will return to the Book of Hosea and its divine questions, and explore their significance from the achieved perspective. But then, because of a specific issue raised by the text, in section *five* I will undertake another general reflection on the existential challenge posed by a genuine impasse, for us, and possibly for God. Then I will return to Hosea 11 for a *final* exploration of its theological overtones. In the course of this multi-phase exploration, I will freely employ a variety of resources not native to technical biblical scholarship. For this I make no apology; the justification, in my view, depends upon the integrity of the result, by which I mean the explication, and not the violation, of the text. One hermeneutical assumption should be disclosed here, or rather a hermeneutical conviction since it has arisen in the course of my experience with texts: I am convinced that the relation between text and interpreter is dialogical.

1.   Relevant Texts

1.11   The first divine question occurs in the context of Hos 6:1–6, of which vv 4–6 read as follows (Mays's translation):

>   (4)   What shall I do with you, O Ephraim?
>   What shall I do with you, O Judah?
>   Your devotion is like morning mist,
>   like dew that soon disappears.
>   (5)   Therefore I have fought (them) with the prophets,

slain them with the words of my mouth;
and so my decision like light goes forth,
(6) that I desire devotion, not sacrifice,
the knowledge of God, rather than burnt offerings.

Mays and Wolff both take this passage as a divine oracular response to the people's liturgical act of penitence portrayed in 6:1-3. Whereas such a liturgical act normally would be expected to evoke an affirmative and encouraging oracle from a cultic spokesman for Yahweh, in this instance the divine word through Hosea takes the form of a question. In this question, says Wolff, "God is pictured struggling with himself (cf. 11:8)" (Wolff:199). Mays comments (96-97),

> The opening questions express a perplexed frustration at Israel's penitence.... Without reserve God discloses the frustration caused by the inconstancy of his people. In the election of Israel Yahweh involved himself in the consequences of their acts. He is the true subject of Israel's history; but he is inextricably by his own free choice a part of the history of which Israel is subject. The history of Israel is the sphere of the struggle and dialogue between man and God—and here the dialogue is like that between husband and fickle wife, father and prodigal son.

1.12 This divine question is followed, in v 5, by an indication of Yahweh's way of dealing with the people. Apparently the verse refers to palpable historical calamities visited upon the people in accordance with prophetic announcements of judgment. Given a "dynamic activistic conception of the word of Yahweh" (Mays:97), the historical agency of judgment in this instance is left unmentioned, in favor of an emphasis upon that divine agency of prophetic speech which the people have failed to heed and which, therefore, through its actualization, will destroy them.

1.21 The second question occurs in the context of Hos 8:1-14 of which we need to quote only vv 5-6 (Mays's translation):

(5) Your bull, O Samaria, is rejected;
my anger burns against them.
How long will they be incapable of innocence?
(6) For what has Israel to do with it?
An artisan made it!
A God it is not!
Yea, splinters shall become
Samaria's bull.

Wolff identifies this question as a lament, by its opening element, and comments that "the lament juxtaposed with the expression of divine wrath indicates how jealous judgment and grieving, expectant love for Israel struggle within Hosea's God" (Wolff:141). Similarly, Mays comments (118-19):

'How long ...' is an interrogatory exclamation used repeatedly in songs of lament....The question which it introduces is rhetorical; the line is really a cry of anguish and sorrow over Israel's inability to live in innocence, free of the deeds that disqualify for relation to God.... In this juxtaposition of lament and burning wrath the God of Hosea discloses the suffering in which the election of Israel has involved him. His anger is not bitter hatred; it is the passion of purpose that will not surrender in spite of frustration and rejection.

1.22   This divine question is followed, in v 6 and following verses, by an indication of Yahweh's way of dealing with the people—a variety of historical calamities construed as divine judgments.

1.31   The third question occurs in the context of Hos 11:1-11, and introduces the central and pivotal section of that long divine address, the section comprising vv 8-9 (my translation):

(8) How can I make you, O Ephraim,
consign you, O Israel,
how can I make you like Admah,
dispose you like Zeboim?
My heart changes itself upon me,
my change of mind grows fervent altogether!
(9) I will not act out my burning anger,
I will not turn to destroy Ephraim—
for I am God and not man,
the Holy One in your midst—
And I will not come to consume.

In this instance the divine question to Israel reaches an extraordinary intensity of passion, in confronting a baffling impasse which calls forth a remarkable disclosure of the interior dynamics of the divine life. Mays characterizes the question in v 8 as a form of "intense ... impassioned self-questioning by Yahweh," in which the divine father "pours out mingled sorrow and love in rhetorical questions which deny just punishment." He goes on to say, "as literary expression of the suffering into which the covenant God has been drawn by Israel's faithfulness, the questions are similar to those in 6:4" (Mays:156). The intensity of the self-questioning arises out of the divine envisagement of a judgment upon Israel so complete and so final as to be analogous to the terrible doom long ago visited upon Admah and Zeboim, cities which along with Sodom and Gomorrah stand in the Old Testament as eminent instances of total and irreversible annihilation. The questioning of such a prospect achieves such passionate intensity because of the long and intimate relationship which has grown up between Yahweh and Israel, a relationship which had its ground in the divine love (11:1) and which took the character of a relation between father and son. Because of this intimate relation, the divine question to Israel is, as Mays says, precisely a *self*-questioning. As I will argue, it is this *self*-questioning which reveals most deeply what it means to say, in Mays's words, that "[Yahweh] is the true subject of Israel's history" who in part by such questions "discloses the suffering in which the election of Israel has involved him" (see Mays's comments on the first two occurrences of the divine question, above §§1.11 and 1.21). That is to say, in view of the nature of the threatened relation between God and people, the question here raised is as much a question of the future of Yahweh as it is a question of the future of Israel. In this instance, now, the disclosed outcome of the divine question is decidedly different from the two earlier instances. Though, in this third passage, divine wrath does in part come to expression in palpable judgment, nevertheless this judgment will not be on the order of Admah and Zeboim, but is qualified by an emphatically reiterated negative resolve (v 9) which leaves both Israel's future and Yahweh's future open to the prospect of eventual reconciliation and restoration. Between the questions of v 8 and the negative resolves of v 9 lie the pivotal, all-important and fatefully significant two lines which Wolff translates

> My heart turns against me,
> my remorse burns intensely

and which Mays translates

> My heart has turned itself against me;
> my compassion grows completely warm.

1.32   Later I shall want to examine the translation of these two lines more closely, and to explore their theological implications in some detail. But at this point it is sufficient to note the contrast which they pose to the contexts of the two earlier divine questions. In 6:4 and in 8:5 the questions are followed purely by references to divine judgment of Israel, that is, to a form of divine action which brings about a decided change in Israel's own experience. But in 11:8-9, while the question still leaves room for judgment (a judgment which is presupposed in vv 10-11), this time there also occurs a form of divine action which transpires completely *within* Yahweh and which has the character of "intra-mural" change or transformation. I would emphasize that this transformation occurs as the outcome of an intense *self*-questioning, to which Israel is made privy through the prophetic word. Again, whereas in 6:5 the divine question issues in a prophetic word which slays the people with a word of judgment, in 11:8-9 the question is contained within a prophetic word which, as Wolff comments, witnesses not so much against Israel and Israel's history as to "the divine love which struggles with Israel *as within itself*" (Wolff:203, italics added). One might say, in other words, that this prophetic word, in the form of this divine question, has to do first of all with the history of *Yahweh*, and only then, and within that *milieu*, with the history of Israel.

2. Asking a Question

2.1   With this introductory look at the divine questions in Hosea, and at some recent commentary on them, I would like now to explore in a general way what it means to ask a question—for a human being, and possibly for God. I am not concerned here with the sort of question that poses a request for information about an already existing state of affairs which happens to be unknown to the questioner. Nor am I concerned with the rhetorical questions (though of the three questions in Hosea, the last two are explicitly described as rhetorical by Mays), except to note that such questions involve that which is well known by the questioner, and so are not intended to elicit an answer, but are posed for rhetorical effect, as a way of drawing the hearer toward what is known by the questioner.

2.2   Rather, I am concerned with what I would call *existential* questions. As I mean this term, an existential question has to do with the fact of being alive. And being alive is a matter of personal growth and becoming, understood as a temporal process through the power of decision exercised in active response to possibilities which stand before one. Such presented possibilities pose themselves as the question of one's existence. What I mean is set out in a well-known passage of a letter by Rainer Maria Rilke, in which he responds to a young man's questions about life. Rilke writes (34–35),

> ... no human being anywhere can answer for you those questions and feelings that deep within them have a life of their own. ... You are so young, so before all beginning, and I want to beg you, as much as I can, dear sir, to be patient toward all that is unsolved in your heart and to try to love the *questions themselves* like locked rooms and like books that are written in a very foreign tongue. Do not now seek the answers, which cannot be given you because you would not be able to live them. And the point is, to live everything. *Live* the questions now. Perhaps you will then gradually, without noticing it, live along some distant day into the answer. Perhaps you do carry within yourself the possibility of shaping and forming as a particularly happy and pure way of living; train yourself to it—but take whatever comes with great trust, and if only it comes out of your own will, out of some need of your inmost being, take it upon yourself and hate nothing.

In this passage, Rilke provides a sensitive description of what it is to experience, to entertain, to enter into the power of an existential question. Such a question is not to be answered, if by answer we mean some piece of information or some notion foreign to the questioner which is brought or drawn toward the questioner who remains stationary. Rather, such a question is to be *lived toward*, in such a way that, in time, the self which one has become is the "answer." The relation between this kind of question and its answer is the relation between the inchoateness of relatively indeterminate possiblility and determinate actuality.

2.3   Moreover, the *power* to live toward such a question arises from the question itself, and this power arises within the person as the question is taken in and entertained attentively. For the power lies in the tension between who and what one *is* at a given point, and who and what one vaguely but importantly senses one may *become*. This connection between the future as question (or hope), and strength for becoming, is illustrated in some of the Hebrew words for hope, in their root meanings and in their usage. *Tiqwâ* can mean either "hope" or "cord." Its root *qwh*, "to wait for," is cognate with Arabic *qawiya*, "to be strong" and *qawwatun*, "strength" or "a strand of rope." Job in 6:11 asks, "What is my strength, that I should wait? / And what is my end, that I should be patient?" Second Isaiah answers (Isa 40:31), "They who wait for Yahweh shall renew their strength." Potential for existence is potency for existence.

2.4   The *question*-character of this potency consists in the fact that one's most significant and encompassing possibilities for becoming never present themselves in clearly determinate form; rather, they are sensed or felt as a directional thrust or pull, which at best may be represented typically through images and symbols. In this respect, existential questions resemble informational questions, in that the one who entertains an existential question cannot say precisely what it is that one is directed toward by means of the question. Indeed, one may suggest a correlation in which question is to answer as faith is to knowledge. But whereas faith sometimes is *criticized* as being a mere belief as to the character of what could just then be known but in fact is not known, so that in such a view faith is a poor and sometimes bad substitute for knowledge; in the sense advocated here, faith is the one possible avenue to knowledge. For faith in this sense concerns that which not only is not yet known but in fact is not yet knowable because it does not yet *exist*—it is the "substance of things hoped for." The point is that questions lead *to* existence by being believed *in*. This connection between faith and existential questions is the central point in William James's classic essay, "The Will To Believe." In this essay, James illustrates his central thesis with reference to questions concerning personal relations, as when one asks another, "Do you like me or not?" In many instances, he points out, the way in which the question is asked, the trust and expectation which is invested in the question, "the previous faith on my part in your liking's existence is in such cases what makes your liking come." So, more generally, he concludes, "there are, then, cases where a fact cannot come at all unless a preliminary faith exists in its coming" (James:23-25). Robert Frost was deeply indebted to James for this understanding of the role of belief, and returned to it again and again in poems, essays and interviews. In one interview he said (Frost in Lathem:271),

> The Founding Fathers didn't believe in the future, . . . they believed it *in*. You're always believing ahead of your evidence. I believe the future *in*. It's coming in by my believing it. You might as well call that a belief in God.

And in the essay, "Education by Poetry," he wrote (Frost in Cox and Lathem:44-46, italics added),

> There are two or three places where we know belief outside of religion. One of them is at the age of fifteen to twenty, in our self-belief. A young man knows more about himself than he is able to prove to anyone. . . . In his foreknowledge he has something that is going to believe itself into fulfillment. . . .
>
> There is another belief like that, the belief in someone else, a relationship of two that is going to be believed into fulfillment. . . .
>
> Then there is a literary belief. Every time a poem is written, every time a short story is written, it is written not by cunning but belief. The beauty, the something, the little charm of the thing to be, *is more felt than known*. . . . No one who has ever come close to the arts has failed to see the difference between things written . . . with cunning and device, and the kind that are believed into existence, that begin in *something more felt than known*. . . .
>
> Now I think—I happen to think—that those three beliefs that I speak of, the self-belief, the love-belief, and the art-belief, are all closely related to the God-belief, that the belief in God is a relationship you enter into with Him to bring about the future.

Understood in this way, existential questions need not present themselves in the form of a *grammatical* question, but simply in whatever form implies a not-completely-determinate, directional possiblity. So far as grammar is concerned, they may take the form of invitation, or suggestion, or enticement, or even command. But all of these specific forms of presentation may be said to have the character of a question, insofar as they initiate a process of response which may (but need not) eventuate in the respondent's becoming that which is not fully determinate until the becoming is complete. To sum up this paragraph, I suggest that an existential question is a source of power for becoming, which power is appropriated and exercised in the mode of active belief. I want now to come at this matter from a somewhat different angle, which I will illustrate with a brief word-play and then relate to biblical modes of thought.

2.5   Already in Latin, *ex(s)istere* appears to have functioned as an intransitive verb meaning "to emerge and stand out, to appear, to exist." But this verb was built from the components *ex* and *sistere* which means "to cause to stand" from *stare* "to stand." This illustrates the notion that what exists, what emerges and stands forth with actuality, does so not out of its own aboriginal power for becoming, but by a power derived from a situation of being *caused* to stand forth. I suggest, then, that what exists stands forth in response to a *call*, in the form of a presented possibility for existence, a call in the form of an existential question. This brief suggestion as to what it means to exist may be taken to explicate two creation texts which are, I believe, not unrepresentative of the Old Testament. Isa 48:13 reads,

> My hand founded the earth
> and my right hand spread out the heavens;
> when I call to them,
> they stand forth together.

And Ps 33:6–9 reads in part,

> By the word of Yahweh the heavens were made,
> and all their host by the breath of his mouth.
> . . .
> For he spoke, and it came to be;
> he commanded, and it stood forth.

According to these passages, existents emerge and stand forth in response to a call. But they are not merely ushered passively and inertly into existence; they are called to appear, to present themselves. And their existence, consequently, is as much a function of their active response as it is of the initiating call. Moreover, I suggest, this active response does not merely confer actuality upon a potentiality whose details are in all respects predeterminate. Rather, the call is always general enough to allow for some contribution of specific detail and originative character on the part of the existent. In other words, the existent partly shapes and determines what and who he or she will become. To give a well-known biblical example, Abraham comes to be who he is through his response to the possibility placed before him by God. This possibility, this awareness of something foreign to his early existence in Haran, something not yet clear to him (and by Gen 15:2 and 16:2 still not clear), something he can only live toward and thereby believe *in*, is Abraham's existential question.

2.6   Now I want to suggest that, as power for becoming, one's existential questions are to be husbanded through descreetly channelled living toward them, and not dissipated through indiscriminate disclosures. For the disclosure of one's own questions to others admits those others into the sphere of one's inner counsel which is the sphere of one's power of becoming. Thus admitted, those others share in that power, for good or ill, and so share in the determination of the final outcome. For example, at least as portrayed in the Gospels, the messianic secret may be shared at the right moment, within a closed circle, but for the time being must be kept from the indiscriminate many, lest the outcome lose all resemblance to the initial possibility.

2.7   When, through a venture of trust, one's question, while yet a question, is fruitfully shared with another, then the outcome will be somewhat different from what it would have been if pursued in solitude. For the other, having been drawn into the sphere of power of one's question, now shares in that power, and so contributes his or her own determinations to the eventual "answer." Such situations at the outset constitute a coming together, a *covenant* in the root sense of that word, in the mode of promise and vow. At the outset, not only does each share in the *power* of the other's question, but each becomes a *part* of the other's question—that is, by the very act of admitting another to one's own question, one allows that question to become re-defined so as to include the other as an element in it. The eventual actualization, the *embodiment* of the question wherein the two become one flesh, has the character of a concrete unification, what one Jewish tradition might call a *yiḥud*, which is coming together or covenanting in the mode of fulfillment. In this unification, each has become a part of the other's answer. So understood, the dialogical character of true covenant relations consists in the sharing of personal power in risk and vulnerability through the mutual disclosure of existential questions. It may be noted, incidentally, that such comings together may arise for the sake of narrow or limited or brief purposes, or for the sake of the most comprehensive and unqualified possibilities in which the total destinies of the parties are at stake.

2.8   There is, of course, another way of disclosing one's existential questions, which avoids the risks of indiscrimination, but which is devoid also of the rewards of mutuality. This sort of disclosure occurs after one's own given question has been lived (believed) into one's own answer. The power for becoming has been exercised and the person has become something at that stage determinate and complete, at least with reference to that question and that phase of the person's existence for which it was powerful. But the power of that question is now spent for that person as a power for *growth*. One must entertain fresh questions, or cease to grow, and instead just lapse into being, through that stationary dance in which one embraces the (now fully determinate) question and repeats the (already achieved) answer. Yet the question which for oneself is spent may still be offered to another, for whom, given the other's stage of growth, it may be a source of genuine power. Of course, there is here no risk for the giver of the spent question. For that person is already complete with reference to this question, and therefore nothing which the other does with the power of this question can any longer affect one's own becoming. I suggest that this is one way to understand the nature of a rhetorical question: it may contribute to the becoming of the one who receives it; but it in no way contributes anything to the one who poses it. One expects no answer to one's rhetorical question. For one already possesses, or rather is, one's answer. In this instance, the other does not enter into one's own sphere of power, to share in the determination of one's own destiny. Rather, the other receives one's no longer needed power. Here, no *covenant* arises.

2.9   The issue toward which this whole discussion has been moving is this: Can God entertain existential questions? Or is God, by virtue of being God, restricted to the entertainment of rhetorical questions only? For classical western thought, including Christian thought generally, the dominant answer is clear: Divinity can ask itself no existential questions. Still less can it share such questions with others. Any questions it may pose to itself or to others are rhetorical. As posed, they may enter into the becoming of others, but not into God's own. For God does not become; God just *is*.

2.10   For process thought generally, the perspective on this issue is quite different. In this perspective, static perfection is not a virtue but a fatal liability. For "even perfection will not bear the tedium of infinite repetition" (Whitehead:258). Rather, the divine perfection is understood to consist in the capacity to change with perfect adequacy in the direction of the divine aim and in league with a fluent world. Indeed, the fluent world itself is understood as receiving its dynamism for change from the God whose own becoming arises out of the divine appetition or "Eros which is the living urge towards all possibilities" (Whitehead:295). The divine eros may be said to consist in the aboriginal power to pose existential questions as means to the advance of the divine life in its own self-enjoyment. This Eros is a *directional* urge, aimed at the enjoyment and the realization of *types* of possibility, rather than at envisagements which are totally specific and determinate.

2.11   But the self-creativity of God does not proceed in solitude. Rather, divine self-creativity goes hand in hand with the emergence of the world in its multifarious forms and occasions of existence. The multifarious existents (the "hosts of heaven and earth") emerge into existence as responses to the disclosed, presented, and so shared divine urge toward novel possibility. This shared divine urge is received locally in the form of what Whitehead calls propositions or "lures for feeling," that is, felt awarenesses of what might be. Such propositions function in the form of the sort of belief of which Frost speaks in the passages quoted above, an awareness of "something, the little charm of the thing to be," an awareness "more felt than known." This awareness often if not always comes to focus in the form of images and metaphors and symbols, which retain the intense feeling of directional lure and indeterminateness with respect to acutualization. Precisely how "what might be" is actualized, and the specific shape and character which the existent takes, depends in some degree upon how the existent exercises the power of becoming which it receives in the form of the presented lure or question.

2.12   With the completion of the occasion of local becoming, that which now exists as a fully determinate finite actuality is received into God, "unto whom are all things." But for process thought, the only way in which anything can meaningfully be said to be received by God is if that entity enters as an ingredient into the divine becoming, where it contributes its finite and local determinateness to the comprehensive determinateness which is the fullness of God in the divine perfection as at that moment. As Rilke puts it (49–50),

> If he is the most perfect, must not the lesser be put *before* him, so that he can choose himself out of fullness and overflow?—Must he not be the last, in order to encompass everything within himself, and what meaning would we have if he, whom we long for, had already been?

2.13   To sum up this brief statement of process thought, in the terms of the primary question of this paper up to now, God whose own life proceeds toward existential questions posed out of the aboriginal fund of the divine appetitive imagination ("I will be who I will be"), discloses those existential questions to that which is not God, thereby at once calling forth new creatures into existence and also sharing with them the divine sphere of power, and God's own becoming. (Compare Mauser:348 and passim.) In this, there is in principle complete mutuality of becoming between God and the hosts which make up the world. It is with God and the world (apart, perhaps, from the specific sexual roles) as depicted in these lines of Lawrence Ferlinghetti:

> then this dame
>   comes up behind me see
>   and says
> You and me could really exist

3.   Aspects of the Old Testament from the Perspective Gained

3.0   What, then, of the Old Testament? Are its portrayals of the divine in its own existence and in its relations with the world patient of interpretation in this perspective? At first one begins to hunt for passages which might be adduced in support of a process versus a classical view of God. Gradually one begins to suspect and finally one becomes convinced that the shoe really belongs on the other foot, and that, in many respects, the Old Testament reads much more naturally and suggestively for theology in a process perspective than otherwise. One massive piece of evidence for this is the hermeneutical difficulties which early synagogue and church faced in attempting to read the Old Testament in the light of theological categories developed under the influence of Greek metaphysics, categories which assumed the impassibility and the immutability of the divine life. The hermeneutical solution was to cry "metaphor" and "anthropomorphism," and in effect to demythologize by converting the "oriental imagery" into philosophical categories. The problem with this practice was not *that* it was attempted, but *how* it was carried out (Mauser)/2/. At certain key points, it seems to me, the conversion did not carry what the text itself implied. Rather, the text was inverted and made to say exactly the opposite of what the metaphors implied. For instance, those passages which portray a God who is internally related to the world, and so capable of feeling and change in response to change in the world, were explained *away*, as accommodations to our human understanding, rather than explored as they stood for their theological implications. By contrast, a process view of things may dispense with many traditional hermeneutical devices designed to "save the [biblical] appearances," since it provides a current thought and language within which we may interpret *along* the metaphorical grain, and not *against* the grain, those Old Testaments portrayals where God's passionality and mutability are either asserted or assumed. Let me adduce a few items in support of this general assertion. The items are admittedly miscellaneous in character, and not very fully developed. The aim here is merely to be suggestive, and to indicate my view that the interpretation of Hosea 11 offered in this paper can be embedded in a congenial interpretation of other aspects of the Old Testament.

3.1   Gen 6:5-8. Two points are noteworthy here. The divine decision for the flood is accounted for, not by appeal to the inscrutable caprice of God, but by appeal to the state of affairs in the world. This world, it may be said, arose as the means to the fulfillment of the divine urge to creation, and to enjoyment of its own creation (Gen 1:4). The enjoyment of the creation, and of the divine self as creator, assumed the "goodness" of that creation (Gen 1:4). But the state of affairs has become so incompatible with the divine creative aims and enjoyment, that the indignant pain which it gives leads God to a change of mind concerning the viability of such a world as a means to those aims. But, secondly, the fact of Noah's existence in righteousness effects a modification in the changing divine purpose. Both with respect to the world in general, and with respect to Noah in particular, the natural conclusion is to suppose that God is internally related to the creation.

3.2   Gen 18:16-33. Again the state of affairs, this time concerning a local region, comes to the point where God purposes to visit that region in justice. In this instance, the way in which Abraham is admitted into the sphere of power of God's question concerning these cities could not be more graphically portrayed. For God has visited Abraham in the persons of three men. Now as God, or these three men, set(s) out toward Sodom, God decides to make Abraham privy to the divine intention, and the reason for this soon becomes apparent. While *two* of the men go on toward Sodom, Yahweh remains standing before Abraham/3/. Of course, the later scribes with philosophical clarity recognized the implications of such a divine action, and in one of their rare deliberate alterations of the text they revised it so as to have Abraham standing before Yahweh. The implications of the original text are clear and momentous, in at least two ways. By standing before Abraham even while proceeding toward Sodom, the text suggests through narrative and dramatic device that God was not finally decided or resolved concerning the future of Sodom. That is to say, the future remained open to at least two types of possibility, and so posed itself as a question for the divine purpose. Further, in remaining before Abraham to see what he would do or say, God drew Abraham into that sphere of decision-making power within which Sodom's fate would be decided. And Abraham's intercession was simply the form which his determining action took.

3.3   It is not too much to suggest that the prophets generally, whether as intercessors or as announcers of the divine word to which they have become privy, are to be understood as standing within the sphere of power of God's questions concerning the future. For the announcement of Yahweh's word, even where it has the grammatical force of a warning, or a seemingly inescapable sentence, at a deeper level has the character of an existential question. As Martin Buber put it (1960b:103–4, italics added),

> The true prophet does not announce an immutable decree. He speaks into the power of decision lying in the moment. . . . The power and ability are given to every man at any definite moment really to take his choice, and by this he shares in deciding about the fate of the moment after this, and this sharing of his occurs in a *sphere of possibility* which cannot be figured either in manner or scale. It is to this personal decision of man with *its part in the power of fate-deciding* that the prophetic announcement of disaster calls.

Of course, it can be objected that the fate which is decided by this power is the fate of the world only, and not the fate of God; so that what we have here is not the disclosure of a divine existential question, but of a question which is existential for human beings but only rhetorical for God. Buber himself, after probing the significance of prophetic activity so sensitively, ends up on a note which, in my view, robs what he has said of its full potential for theological reflection, and betrays his education in the classical philosophical and hermeneutical tradition. For, in turning to a discussion of the Book of Jonah, with its paradigmatic dramatization of the dialogue between humankind and God within the sphere of shared possibility, and its portrayal of human repentence followed by divine repentence, Buber writes (1960b:104),

> Human and divine turning correspond the one to the other; not as if it were in the power of the first to bring about the second, such ethical magic being far removed from Biblical thought, but—"Who knows."

This sentence is an astoundingly clear example of how classical modes of thought about God can bewitch the otherwise sound hermeneutical perceptions of a sensitive student of the Bible. For it is clear that the "ethical magic" really is on the other foot! What else can we call it but magic, when we have two actions in temporal sequence, such that the second *appears* to follow from the first, and yet there is no *discoverable* causal relation and indeed there is said to *be* no causal relation; and nevertheless the moral and existential climate of urgency indicates that we are to attend to both actions *as though* they had something to do with one another? In the absence of any identifiable or conceivable causal relation, simply to introduce the phrase "correspond to one another" is to wave the wand of magic incantation over a process which one cannot or will not venture to understand. One might pause to compare Jonah with Jer 18:5-11 where the causal connection between human turning and divine turning is unmistakably drawn. Perhaps one goes too far in contrasting the Jonah passage with that in Jeremiah, by suggesting that in the former instance the uncertainty as to ethical dialogue between heaven and earth exists in the mind and on the lips of a pagan king, while in the latter instance the explicit assertion of the existence of such a dialogue arises in an inner-covenantal context. Surely the conclusion which we must draw, if we are not to destroy the force of the passages altogether, is that humankind is privy to the sphere of power by which the future is decided. But this future is not just the future of the world; it is also the future of God. For when human actions bring about a change in God's purposes for the world, they thereby bring about a change in God. For there is little if anything that is more definitive of one's own inner existence than one's purposes, and it makes no sense to speak of God's (or anyone's) purposes as external to oneself.

3.4   The capacity of human beings to share in the determination of the life of God is shown in a number of other ways, of which only a few may briefly be alluded to here. *Item*: In the OT the act of blessing, whether undertaken by God to humankind, or by one person to another, is portrayed as an efficacious enrichment of the one blessed by the very power of being which quickens the one who blesses. Now, in worship Israel is said to bless God (e.g., Ps 103). On what biblical or other basis do we decide that the context of worship, and the nature in this instance of the recipient, gives blessing a meaning different from that which it otherwise has? Is it not at least worth considering the possibility that the significance of the act of blessing generally indicates the true character and importance of blessing in the act of worship? *Item*: Ps 50 (and compare Ps 51) has God repudiate sacrificial offerings. On what basis? That God has no need of bulls and goats? Or is it that, as the text asserts, bulls and goats are already God's but that (as the whole psalm implies) there *is* a sacrifice which God looks for and which is *not* God's unless it is *offered*—the offering of human thanksgiving together with a life of covenant integrity? It may indeed be *ḥesed* which God desires, and not sacrifice (Hos 6:6). But this suggests that it is not the logic of sacrifice which is in question, but its content. The verb *ḥapeṣ*, "delight in, take pleasure in" (Hos 6:6) indicates that it lies in human power to offer *ḥesed* for, or to withhold it from, the enrichment of the divine experience. *Item*: One is bidden to love God and to love one's neighbor as oneself. On what basis does one understand the second action to contribute to the neighbor's well-being, while one demurs from understanding the first to contribute to God's? Surely the ultimate biblical motive for ethical existence is not human well-being—important though that motive is—but God's pleasure. But what does it mean for God to take pleasure in the lives of God's creatures? Even if it be objected that God's concern for human ethical existence arises out of concern for *human* welfare, and not out of a concern for the divine self-enjoyment, this only pushes the issue one step further back. The point remains that one or another kind of human behavior toward another human being can and does bring joy or pain to the divine care for the world. But that care is not external to the divine life; it is intrinsic to the divine character. And the moral history of the world is etched upon, or rather etches, the contours of the biography of the divine care, for which not even the welfare of the foreigner or the eunuch is ever forgotten (Isa 56:3–5). *Item*: God not only works and rests according to the divine self-determined "schedule" (Gen 1:1–2:3; Exod 31:17), but God can be made to labor and become weary under the burden of a people which misuses the power shared with it (Isa 1:14; 43:24). *Item*: The divine life can bind itself to humankind by an oath concerning the fulfillment of a promise, such that the violation of that oath will rend the divine life in two (Gen 15:7–21, especially v 17).—Note that it is not Abraham who passes between the divided parts, but a numinous being. Or is it that the two items, the smoking firepot and the flaming torch, represent God and Abraham, as though even a promissory covenant called for *some* kind of human participation if only in the form of trust?—Insofar as the self-binding has to do with a future which is open but directed, that self-binding constitutes the entertainment, the appropriation and the husbanding of the power of the divine Eros in one of its forms; and insofar as that self-binding is undertaken in the presence of a human being, that person is drawn into the sphere of power of the oath, and indeed becomes a part of the very question itself.

3.5   It is sometimes said that, in contrast to the gods of the Ancient Near East, "Yahweh has no myth concerning his life." (The source of this sentence is lost to me.) The intention of such a saying is to take note of an obvious difference between the divine myths of the Ancient Near East and the divine-human epic of the OT. But I suggest the difference is thereby misconstrued. Insofar as the myths concern the lives of the gods, they do so by portraying the mutually internal relations between the gods, and the vicissitudes of their several life stories arising out of those internal relations. What strikes one about these myths is that, while the gods affect one another by existing together within that "sphere of possibility" (to use Buber's term) and sphere of shared power which constitutes the Divine Council, and while their actions affect humankind and so constitute existential questions, yet the myths give little space to the actions of human beings as significant or determinative for the gods. While it is true that human ritual action and prayer are assumed to be efficacious in winning the response of the gods, it does seem significant that, in the myths themselves, taken as portrayals of the fundamental character of things, little or no place is made for human determination of the course of events by their interactions. There is a long but direct line from the ancient gods and their monopoly on the power of fate-deciding, to contemporary determinisms arising from a consideration of the workings of natural laws. By contrast, in the OT the whole story has to do with the interrelations between Yahweh and the *human* community, while so-called encounters between Yahweh and the other gods appear around the edges of the drama. But it is not as though myth has been pushed to one side, and the life of God rendered totally opaque and invisible. I suggest that just the reverse has happened. Humankind has been drawn into the myth and now shares the stage with divinity. The sphere of power is no longer only somewhere else, *in illo tempore*, across the plains or on the summit of the cosmic mountain or at the sources of the double deep: it is that public and present world which humans inhabit. The whole OT is the myth concerning Yahweh's life.

3.61   Finally, the very notion of covenant, which by common consent is fundamental to the OT, involves the mutuality of shared power by the mutual disclosure of existential questions between God and humankind. There is an intrinsic resemblance, which spans the difference in magnitude, tone and importance between

> You and me could really exist

and

> You shall be my people
> and I will be your God.

In respect to the Sinai covenant, it is customary to emphasize the unilateral and non-parity character of the divine-human relation therein established. But, comparative models notwithstanding, and if the biblical writer be allowed the freedom to re-fashion such models to accord with Israel's own religious experience, some features of the Sinai covenant tradition call for re-consideration. For example, Exod 19:3-10, read closely, sounds less like the unilateral imposition of a treaty than the offer of covenant relation—an offer which is presented for the people's acceptance. And, more strikingly, the climactic act of covenant sealing, in 24:6-8, is exactly symmetrical and mutual: (a) blood is sprinkled on the altar (that earthly proxy for God); (b) God's words are read; (b¹) the people voice their response to God's words; (a¹) blood is sprinkled on the people. One notes the chiastic structure of the text, here peculiarly suited to a portrayal of a covenanting bond encompassing both parties. One notes, further, that the words of the covenanting parties are exchanged within the frame of that symbolic act of the most profound significance—the blood which marks *both* parties. Whatever else that act signifies, surely it signifies that the claims of the covenant go to the very heart of the life (and the death for covenant infidelity) of both parties. Again, if one compares this passage, so read, with the passage in Genesis 15 (see §3.4 above) where both parties are symbolically represented as passing between the parts of the slain creatures, perhaps the differences between basic covenant-types in the OT should be taken as differences in emphasis, and not pressed into a stereotypical dichotomy.

3.62   What it means for Israel to have Yahweh as her God, is an open question; and it is likewise an open question for Yahweh as to what it means to have Israel as the people of Yahweh. It is within the sphere of this all-encompassing open question that all local and specific questions arise, including the three which are explicitly posed in Hosea and to which we may now finally turn.

4.   Divine Questions in Hosea from the Perspective Gained

4.1   In Buber's words, the prophetic word in Hosea, taken as a whole, may be said to have been spoken "into the power of decision lying in the moment," which in this instance was the historical situation in which Israel existed at that time. This word did not function to "announce an immutable decree." How *could* it, since long ago already Yahweh had admitted Israel (as, in one way or another, the whole creation) into the "sphere of possibility," the "power of fate-deciding"? The power of action arising out of Yahweh's own existential questions was no longer solely in Yahweh's hands so as to issue unilateral immutable decrees. Rather, this word functioned to elicit a *turning*. But it became apparent that Israel's own defective behavior with its consequences made such a turning to Yahweh increasingly difficult and unlikely, as Israel became "increasingly bound to that behavior until eventually it [was] enslaved (5:4a; 9:10b, 16a; 13:1f)" (Ward:401). The prophet's announcement of disaster was delivered into such an extreme situation as a last possibility for touching "the innermost soul," in order "to evoke the extreme act: the turning to God" (Buber, 1960b:104). But this means that, as such, Hosea's announcement of doom, for all its declarative mode of address, at a deeper level had the character of a *question*, as if to ask: What will you, now, make of this imminent probability, which threatens to be inescapable, and which *will* be inescapable if present tendencies are without alteration merely extended into the future?

4.2   This deeper, questioning character of the prophetic word of Hosea as a whole comes to the surface, like stone outcroppings in the foothills of Colorado, in the three explicit questions which punctuate the divine address to Israel. In these questions, the true force and purpose of the total address becomes evident. It is not that the announcements of disaster are a mere *bluff*. For disaster is an all-too-likely outcome. The specific trajectories of historical momentum which combine to define Israel's situation of crisis, drive toward the doom which is announced, a doom which at one and the same time Israel calls down upon herself and Yahweh visits upon her. But the future is never completely foredoomed. There is always a margin for decision, a margin for negotiability within which both Israel and Yahweh must find the way forward. Granted, then, that these divine questions are "a cry of anguish and sorrow over Israel's inability to live in innocence . . . ," and as such, a disclosure of "the suffering in which the election of Israel has involved [God]" (Mays:119), one may ask: What is the purpose of such a passionate disclosure—or perhaps one should say, of such a disclosure of passion? Is it not to speak, in this most vulnerable and therefore perhaps most persuasive and finally efficacious mode, into Israel's power of fate-deciding, and thereby—who knows?—evoke a turning? Is it not, perhaps, to punctuate the announcement of doom in such a way as to show that, precisely in their declarative force, these announcements have as their aim to jolt Israel out of the somnambulistic assurance of its wrong-headed ways, and to bring Israel back to the awareness that it stands within that sphere of becoming which it properly shares with Yahweh? But if this be the case, then the questions are not rhetorical, but existential.

4.3   The questions show Yahweh placed before an impasse which seemingly can be overcome only by choosing one of two ways forward, either of which is unthinkable: either to execute the righteous judgment of God in that overflowing of wrath which would break off the covenant relation; or to continue to overlook Israel's persistent subversion of God's aims, and thereby (as surely as by judgmental severance of relations) to fail to bring Yahweh and Israel to that "answer," that fulfillment, implied in the divine existential question which initiated the covenant relationship. How is this impasse to be negotiated, without loss to the divine aim?

4.4   According to Wolff and Mays, the impasse is overcome in the course of a *conflict* within the divine life itself which is resolved through the overthrow of divine wrath by divine compassion or love, intensified or spurred on by divine remorse (Wolff). Mays translates the last two lines of v 8:

> My heart has turned itself against me;
> my compassion grows completely warm.

On these lines he comments in part (157),

> To be like Admah and Zeboiim is to exist only as a memory of swift and final calamity. In face of such a fate for Israel Yahweh has become like a man in whose self-consciousness wrath and love battle with each other. His heart, the seat of consciousness and will, assumes a hostile position against the punishment which he has already announced (9:6, 11–13; 10:8, 14f). Compassion, the tender emotion which parents feel toward the helpless child, grows increasingly strong and displaces wrath. . . . Yahweh speaks of himself in the human genre to disclose in emotional terms that his election of Israel is stronger than their sin.

This is a bold interpretation indeed, one which envisions the divine life at odds within itself, such that (Mays:157)

> Yahweh speaks as a man incapable of action because of his divided feelings, caught by the growing power of desire and emotion which oppose what he must do.

This boldness, however, is then blunted by Mays's cautionary recollection of the metaphorical mode of this biblical portrayal of Yahweh, which should remind us that "Hosea's many anthropomorphisms are meant as interpretive analogies, not as essential definitions." But unless we are simply to *replace* such analogies with essential definitions derived from elsewhere (for example, with the essential definitions of a static divine perfection involving divine impassibility and immutability), how do we move from metaphor to reality? Is it not by following the thrust of the analogy? For all their manifold richness of overtone and allusion, metaphors at their center do imply one thing and not another; and the most natural procedure is to take metaphor as adumbrating an essential character which is analogous to the metaphoric vehicle, and not contrary to it. When Mays goes on to say, "He is wrathful and loving *like man*, but *as* God," I take him to be on firm ground. But I will propose that the difference which his assertion alludes to is to be identified otherwise than as he suggests. First, however, let us consider what Wolff has to say on these two lines. Wolff translates,

> Mein Herz kehrt sich gegen mich,
> meine Reue entbrennt mit Macht,

which is rendered in the English version of his commentary,

> My heart turns against me,
> my remorse burns intensely.

He comments on these lines (201, italics added):

> Yahweh's will is directed against himself, i.e., against his wrath (v 9a). In the phrase "my heart turns against me,". . . '*ālay* . . . has a hostile sense. The rarely used word "remorse" (*niḥumim*) . . . emphasizes *the turning point* in Yahweh's will attested in v 8. . . . His remorse (over his wrathful intention to judge) "grows hot," i.e., it provokes him and dominates him. . . . Again and again we see the God of Hosea in conflict with himself over Israel.

Apropos the immediately following lines in v 9, Wolff goes on to say (202),

> It is important to note that the concept of Yahweh's holiness, appearing only once in Hosea, provides the foundation not for his judging will but for his saving will, to which he had committed himself from the very beginning of Israel's saving history.

And in this context he also says (202),

> God proves himself to be God and Holy One in Israel in that he, unlike men, is independent of his partner's actions. Remaining completely sovereign over his own actions, he is not compelled to react. . . . The final period of the nation's history is not to be dominated by the consequences of Israel's deeds (vv 5–7); rather, the future will be determined [sic] by Yahweh's decision to let his love rule.

This interpretation does take the figurative language with unflinching seriousness, and attempts to draw consequences for theology which preserve the implications of the figures. Wolff says later (203),

Of great theological significance in this chapter is its disclosure that Israel's election and guidance is founded upon God's love (vv 1, 4); this love is not some inconstant characteristic but proves to be the incomparable, holy essence of God himself. Yahweh cannot set aside his love just as he cannot set aside his divinity.

The clear implication of this last passage, that unlike the divine love God's wrath is an "inconstant characteristic" and therefore not an element in God's "holy essence," is explicitly stated in a comment upon another passage, where Wolff writes (114), "His wrath is to be distinguished from his essence, as a tool is distinguished from the master craftsman who uses it" (compare, less explicitly, Mays:90). If this distinction is correct, then it is clear that God may set aside wrath without setting aside divinity. But then the internal conflict, after all, cannot be much of a struggle, for it is an uneven and foredoomed match between God's holy essence and some inconstant characteristic or occasional instrument. Indeed, in this case the portrayal of God as " a man incapable of action because of his divided feelings" would have to be said to be overdrawn, or to be merely a rhetorical—a misleading rhetorical—device pointing to no genuine impasse in God. But it is doubtful that the wrath of God is to be given so slight a status in the divine life. It may be that God is *slow* to anger and *abounding* in steadfast love (Ps 103:8); but this difference by itself does not place the two feelings upon a different basis within the divine nature/4/. To set aside wrath is as essentially problematical for Yahweh in the OT as to set aside love. Yet, in summing up the commentary of Wolff and Mays on this point, it may be said that this is how they see Yahweh overcoming the impasse. In so overcoming it, Wolff asserts, God in sovereign freedom and power acts independently of the human partner's actions, toward which God is not compelled to react. Now, such an interpretation is, in Wolff's words, "of great theological significance"—indeed! The significance is one with which I would have such difficulty that I should have to resolve my own mind on the matter by a process such as they ascribe to God, by a denial of one part of me for the sake of another part—were I able in the first place to accept the translations of the text upon which their interpretations are based. But the translations, in my judgment, are forced and do not follow the most natural meaning of the text. It will be necessary, then, to examine the linguistic elements of these two lines in some detail, before continuing with this hermeneutical exploration.

4.5   The Hebrew text reads as follows:

nehpak ʿālay libbî
yaḥad nekmĕrû niḥûmay

Now it is acknowledged freely that the opening verb can be used to refer to polemical actions of "overthrow." This is the case primarily with the simple, or *qal*, stem of the verb, as in all instances of the cognate *mahpēkâ* which always (6 times) refers to the overthrow of Sodom and Gomorrah. Also, the *niphal* stem (which is the stem in Hos 11:8) functions once in the passive voice to describe the (projected) overthrow of Nineveh in Jonah 3:4. Wolff's comments (201) assume that because of the mention of Admah and Zeboiim in v 8, this aspect of the meaning of *nehpak* must be, or at any rate is, dominant in its occurrence in the line in question. Certainly, given the plurisignative way poetic language does its work, one can hardly fail to hear such overtones which perhaps function to create tensive contrast. But the attempt to elevate these overtones to the status of primary meaning breaks down. Let me try to show this by quoting again a comment by Wolff: "Yahweh's will is directed against himself, i.e., against his wrath." In this sentence, Wolff asserts in a footnote, "Yahweh's will" is identified with "my heart"—presumably indicating his true and deepest and essential purpose. The pronoun "me" Wolff takes to refer to "himself, i.e., . . . his wrath (v 9a)." Now, in order for Wolff's interpretation to work, so as to have the verb *nehpak* somehow function with the overtones of the polemical uses of this root, we have to imagine that Yahweh's (saving) will overthrows the divine wrath. We could do this if the subject of the verb, *libbî* = "my heart/will," governed a *transitive* form of the verb so as to yield a rendering "my will overthrows me" or the like. Or we could do this if the *niphal* stem which is in fact used here were to be taken in the passive voice (as in Jonah 3:4) with "me" as subject, to give "I am overthrown by my heart/will" or the like. But the text allows neither of these possibilities. It does not allow us to understand the verb *nehpak* as indicating a polemical relationship between "my heart" on the one hand and "me" on the other, with the heart the victor. Among polemical options allowed by the syntax, the best we could imagine would be a reading, "my heart is overthrown upon me," in which case the actor, and victor, is a third party not identified. If we take *nehpak* as reflexive, we might try to imagine some sort of analog of a civil war—"my heart overthrows itself . . ."—but there is no other instance of such a connotation of this verb in the reflexive voice.

4.6   But the verb *hāpak*, both in the *qal* and in the *niphal* stem, also has another very common meaning in the reflexive voice, which fits the present context much more naturally, and which carries sufficient dramatic force to sustain and even to provide a climax for the emotional intensity to which Hosea 11 has been building since the first verse. That meaning describes some kind of *change*. In such instances, the verb describes a qualitative change affecting the totality of the entity to which it refers. Thus, for instance, it may refer to a change in the color of one's physiological awareness (1 Sam 4:19), a change in the quality of one's pervasive emotional state (Jer 31:13), or a change in one's attitude toward another (Ps 105:25)/5/. The verb may also describe a change in the total character of a person. This is implied in the analogy of Jer 13:23, and it is made explicit in 1 Sam 10:6, "and you shall be turned into another man," a transformation described in 10:9 in these words: "And God gave him another heart." This last text collocates the verb *hāpak* and the noun *heart* in a portrayal of non-polemical change. All of these usages indicate the naturalness with which the verb *hāpak* may be taken to refer to a change of heart. This meaning for the line in question in Hosea 11 is supported by the preposition which accompanies the verb, as we shall now try to show.

4.7   Wolff analyzes the preposition *'ālay* as having a "hostile sense." Again, it is granted that this preposition often does occur in polemical contexts with the meaning "upon = against." Yet this is hardly the most natural meaning in the present context. For the word is also used freqently in descriptions of changes in the inner, emotional state of a person. In such instances, the force of the preposition "upon" is to portray the subject as in some manner experiencing or undergoing one's own changing state, so that one is the recipient who "suffers" this change (BDB:753, II.1.d). In some instances of this usage, the relation between the object of the preposition and the action in the verb is complex, so that somehow the subject is both *agent* and *recipient*. An instructive example, in which the *niphal* stem occurs with reflexive force, is Neh 5:7 *wayyimālēk libbî 'ālay* (grammatically and semantically an exact parallel to *nehpak 'ālay libbî*): "my heart took counsel upon me," or "I took counsel with myself." It need hardly be pointed out that here no polemical overtones are present in the preposition. Other examples in which the subject is both agent and recipient of action are Ps 42:5, "I will pour out my soul upon me" (on which see note 4), and Job 10:1, "I will let loose my complaint upon me." In short, then, the preposition in such instances gives vivid expression to that awareness which accompanies certain intensely felt actions in which the actor through his or her own action undergoes changes. So then, I propose (in basic agreement with Wilhelm Rudolph) that the most natural translation of this line is "my heart changes itself upon me"/6/.

4.8   Parallel to this line, the Hebrew text proceeds to say:

Yaḥad nikměrû niḥûmay

The verb *kāmar*, which occurs only in the *niphal* stem, means "to grow intensely warm, or hot." In three of its four occurences in the OT it describes a surge of positive feeling (see Gen 43:30; 1 Kgs 3:26, where the feeling arises in relation to one's child or one's brothers). What is it that surges fervently in Hos 11:8? It is *niḥûmay*, which may be translated "my compassions" or the like. Wolff, however, understands the word to signify the *intransitive* rather than the *transitive* aspect of its root meaning/7/. This is clear both from his translation "remorse" (*Reue*) and from his comment that this "rarely used word . . . emphasizes the *turning point* in Yahweh's will attested in v 8" (italics added). That is to say, I take the two locutions, *nehpak libbî 'ālay* and *niḥûmay*, as synonymous, and as referring to a change or transformation which takes place within Yahweh. Rhetorically, what we have in the two lines is a first line which sets forth in *clausal* form the theme of the change in God; and a second line which recapitulates that clausal statement in *nominal* form—*niḥûmay*—and then contributes additional characterization of that change: it *grows fervent*. Moreover, it grows fervent in a particular manner, a manner characterized by the emphatically positioned adverb *yaḥad*, a word which is of great significance for our discussion.

4.9   The root *yḥd* occurs in verbal form only rarely in the OT. In the *qal* stem it occurs twice, in the negative (Gen 49:6; Isa 14:20), to indicate that someone is not to *join* a group of people in their particular mode of assembly. In the *piel* stem it expresses the prayer that Yahweh might *unite* the worshipper's *heart* to fear his name (Ps 86:11). These few occurrences show that the meaning has to do with togetherness, or existence in concert. By far the majority of the occurrences of this root take the form of an adverb, either *yaḥad* (as in the present instance), or *yaḥdāw* which carries the basic meaning "together"/8/. In a large number of instances, the adverb characterizes a situation in which a number of persons come together to take counsel for some specific purpose (e.g., Josh 9:2; 11:5; Ps 2:2; 71:10; Isa 45:21). The adverb functions to indicate not just their physical togetherness but their unanimity in counsel and purpose which constitutes them as an assembly (*qāhāl*), an intimate privy council (*sōd*) (Gen 49:6). The covenanting /9/ character of such a coming together is shown in Ps 83:6 (5 EVV):

> they conspire *with one accord*,
> against thee they make *a covenant*.

One might say that in such contexts the adverb describes the process whereby "the many become one." The unity thereby achieved arises with reference to some *purpose* to which all are privy and with which all are in accord. The root also describes an analogous process as it may occur within an individual. (Indeed, it is highly suggestive that the form *yāḥîd*, which most often means "only, only one, solitary," can occur as a synonym for *nepeš* or self, in Ps 22:21 and 35:17). The prayer in Ps 86:11, "unite (*yaḥēd*) my heart to fear thy name," clearly is to be connected to the injunction to love Yahweh with all one's heart, and to the quality of inner integrity or undividedness expressed in the phrases *tām lēb* (Gen 20:5, 6) and *lēb šālēm* (1 Kgs 8:61 and often). One may consult also 1 Chr 12:17 /10/.

4.10   We are in a position, now, to appreciate the significance in Hos 11:8 of the plural form *niḥûmay* and the ingressive force of the verb *nikměrû*, as the noun and verb are qualified by *yaḥad*. The change which takes place in Yahweh is "wholehearted." All the components of the divine life—including, specifically, both the divine wrath and the divine love—grow fervently together in the new purpose to which the divine life becomes resolved:

> My heart changes itself upon me,
> my change of mind grows fervent altogether!

4.11 What the two lines together describe, then, is a process of change which takes place within Yahweh, a change in which the dilemma is dealt with in such a manner that the outcome is an undivided feeling and attitude and purpose, a change in which Yahweh is both initiator and outcome. It is by *this* means, and not by a divided purpose in which one element dominates and overrules the other, that the impasse is negotiated. Moreover, as I shall argue in a moment, it is this difference which provides the basis for the assertion of an emphatic contrast between God and humankind in vs 9. How, then, may we interpret this change and understand this contrast? Since the contrast makes implicit appeal to the way humans characteristically act in such impasses, it is appropriate (indeed, one may say that the text with assertorial lightness directs us) to reflect upon such human action in general.

5. The Existential Challenge Posed by a Genuine Impasse

5.1 The general phenomenon of human decision-making shows that all too often such an impasse is resolved by choosing in favor of one or another of the components of deep feeling. The tragedy is that such a decision results in something less than existential wholeness—the decision cuts off a palpable and organic part of the actual situation, including an organic part of the deciding self. For what has happened is that one component feeling has been identified as relatively evil, and the other component feeling as relatively good, and the evil has been rejected and the good adopted. But since, in the case of a genuine impasse, each component arises as a momentum of personal energy, a concrete determinate power of action which makes its own efficacious claims on the total situation, to choose one over against the other is to lose part of the total power and efficacy of the situation. And insofar as one is internally related to that situation, this means to lose part of one's own concrete self/11/. One may, after a fashion, negotiate the impasse and enter into the kingdom, but one does so minus an eye or a hand or a foot, or (*vide* Origen) something else. Such a choice may, in such situations, be the best thing that one as a human being can carry through, and as such it partly gives the human situation its character of tragedy.

5.2 But even for the human finiteness in its tragic weakness there is the challenge, as Buber argues in *Good and Evil*, not to reject the evil impulse (the *yeṣer hārā'*) in favor of the good impulse (the *yeṣer haṭōb*), but to unify all the impulses in an act which sustains one's relation to the total passional situation and at the same time to the fundamental direction of one's life. Buber's development of the Talmudic doctrine of the two urges is worth introducing here at some length, for the light it may shed on Hos 11:8–9, as well as for the possible extension which the general argument of this paper may indicate for that doctrine. Buber writes (1953:94–97),

> In the creation of man, the two urges are set in opposition to each other. The Creator gives them to man as his two servants which, however, can only accomplish their service in genuine collaboration. The 'evil urge' is no less necessary than its companion. . . . Man's task, therefore, is not to extirpate the evil urge, but to reunite it with the good. . . . Man is bidden . . . : 'Love the Lord with all thine heart,' and that means, with thy two united urges. The evil urge must also be included in the love of God[,] thus and thus only does man become once more as he was created: 'very good.' . . . But how is the evil urge to be prevailed upon to permit this to happen to it? Why, it is nothing but a crude ore, which must be placed in the fire to be moulded. . . .

Buber goes on to characterize the two urges thus:

> the evil 'urge' as passion . . . which, left to itself, remains without direction and leads astray, and the 'good urge' as pure direction, in other words, as an unconditional direction, that towards God.

And he concludes,

> To unite the two urges implies: to equip the absolute potency of passion with the one direction that renders it capable of great love and of great service. Thus and not otherwise can man become whole.

I will interrupt these extended quotations at this point, to suggest that, within the perspective of this paper, the "unconditional direction" of which Buber speaks may be interpreted in terms of the fundamental divine existential question, by admission to the sphere of power within which humankind receives its high calling and task. Of course, Buber confines this task of unification (what this Jewish tradition calls *yiḥud*) to human beings, and limits the scope of what is to be united to the created world; and he explicitly repudiates the notion of "this unification as taking place 'in' God" (1966:215)/12/. As will shortly be seen, the notion which he repudiates is here adopted, and will be the very meaning claimed to be implicit in Hos 11:8–9. Meanwhile, one further quotation may be introduced (1953:130–31):

> By decision we understand, not a partial, a pseudo decision, but that of the whole soul. . . . Good can only be done with the whole soul. It is done when the soul's rapture, proceeding from its highest forces, seizes upon all the forces and plunges them into the purging and transmuting fire, as into the mightiness of decision. Evil is lack of direction and that which is done in it and out of it as the grasping, seizing, devouring, compelling, seducing, exploiting, humiliating, torturing and destroying of what offers itself. Good is direction and what is done in it; that which is done in it is done with the whole soul, so that in fact all the vigour and passion with which evil might have been done is included in it.

These quotations indicate the challenge which is posed whenever a genuine impasse arises in the path of existence, that is, in the path of becoming. The challenge is not merely to sustain or maintain oneself, nor merely to restore a unity as it previously existed, but rather to forge a wholeness which, since it must encompass new elements including impulses and efficacious passions which have arisen in the new situation, is a *new* wholeness. If in the process humankind becomes once more as created—"very good"—it becomes clear that in this process humankind participates in creation.

5.3   Now, in a process perspective, I suggest, the existential task of *yiḥud*—the task of holistic becoming through unification of one's world—characterizes not only, nor eminently, human life, but first of all and eminently the life of God. For the divine unity is not a static but a dynamic perfection. This dynamic perfection arises out of God's internal relatedness to the world. God (after Rilke's words quoted above in §2.12) chooses the divine self out of fullness and overflow "in order to encompass everything within himself." The unity of God is realized ever afresh through that sovereign freedom and power whereby, in each new occasion of the divine relation to the world, God draws the world in all its multifarious determinateness into the divine life, passionately conforms the divine life perfectly to these finite forms of determinateness, and yet does so in such a manner as to sustain the aboriginal *direction* (Buber) indicated by the divine Eros, God's own aboriginal existential question. In this view, the sovereign freedom and power is not demonstrated in the divine independence of the human partner's actions, to which God is not compelled to react (Wolff). Quite the opposite! God's sovereign freedom and power emerge in the process by which, having conformed with perfect passional sympathy to the actions of the human partner, and thereby, so to speak, having the divine agenda set by the human partner's actions (for what else could genuine dialogue between God and humankind mean?), God goes on to act in a manner which sustains both the total relationship with the human partner, in all its concrete particularity, and the aboriginal divine purpose.

5.4   This process of "choosing" involves struggle, wherein the various mutually discordant components and vectors of purposive energy in the world are drawn into an ideal unification or harmonization. As discordant and incompatible among themselves in the world, the component energies in the world tend—with varying vectors of efficacious momentum—toward their own destruction. Since their discordancies arise out of their own several decisions, this destruction or doom may be said to be brought upon themselves. But this doom or wrath is not merely "the way the world works," as though wrath were to be understood solely as a kind of "natural law" of moral retribution originally ordained by God but now operating purely in the world and externally to God or with God external to it. Rather, this wrath is quite appropriately, and I would argue most properly, to be understood as the wrath of God/13/. For (in my understanding) God receives the world into the divine life initially without qualification, aberration, or remainder ("unto him are *all* things"; Rom 11:36). In the technical language of Whitehead, God makes no negative prehensions. God carefully—fully and with care—receives every quantum of energy and emotion and impulse and action that arises in the world, in and with its peculiar quality of feeling and direction of aim, into the divine life, by God's own conformal or passional power. Therein God allows the divine life to be determined by the multifarious determinatenesses of the world. The divine life makes these passions its own—God owns them. In this way, the wrath which arises in the world in the form of mutually discordant, eccentrically-misdirected efficacious actions tending to the destruction of some region or all of the world, *becomes* the wrath of God. Or rather, it gives concrete shape and existential texture to that wrath which, as essential element in God, is the settled divine disposition against all which works merely against the divine will and aim for itself and the world. At this point, the complete fact is the wrath of *God*; and it is only by a retrograde abstraction that we may think of it as wrath operating by some kind of natural law in the world. God's wrath, then, as a variable, historical experience, arises from the world through God's own perfect conformal feeling of the world. There is an analogy here with human experience, in which wrath arises within one, not as a deliberate intention, but as a passion which acts upon one. Were God merely to exclude or reject or deny any least such wrathful feeling, the divine life would to that extent fail to know and relate to that part of the world with perfect adequacy. But on the other hand, merely to "know the world as it is," and to acquiesce in its settled determinateness and its vector energies, and so to allow its vectors to determine the divine future, would be to lose sight of the aboriginal divine aim within the sphere of which the relation with the world has been established and pursued. To lose *either one* of them—either the totality of the determinate vectors of the world inclusive of its wrathful components, or the aboriginal divine aim of which the world has been made a constituent member—would be, I suggest against Wolff, to "set aside his divinity" in favor of one or other of what would by themselves become demonic forces/14/. Therefore, an act of *transformation* is called for, by means of which the disparate ingredients in the divine wrath are incorporated into a wider, deeper vision and to which they may ultimately contribute.

5.5   It is important to note here that this transformation does not imply a material change in the elements of the world themselves. God does not tamper with the results of our decisions, so as to undo what we have done and thereby in effect rob our power of decision of its reality and its importance. What God's transformation does imply may be adumbrated in two aspects. First, it implies a transformation in the specific forms of relevant possibility by which the aboriginal divine Eros may achieve its aims. That is to say, the transformation is something which occurs in the mode of imaginative vision with God. The transformation effects an imaginative reconciliation of the world within God, by means of which the unity of the divine life is a *new* unity. This unity, however, is not something thereby actualized. It is a unity which, imaginatively achieved in God, becomes God's will for the world—that is to say, it remains to be rendered concrete and actual through the world's doing of God's will. This imaginative unification thus constitutes the new form of the divine existential question. Were God to render concrete such a unity, to actualize it, by solitary action, we should have to take any questions arising for the world out of this new situation as being only *rhetorically* posed for the world by God (see above, §2.8). But in the perspective here being argued such is not the case. Rather, this new form of the question, this imaginative vision, is then offered to the world, so that the world is drawn into its sphere of power. It is offered to the world as a translucent garment of possibility which clothes/15/ all the determinate elements and vector forces of the world, including the components tending toward wrath. The garment does not itself change the settled world. Rather, the garment, by a kind of refraction which may alter the world's vision for itself, opens the way for the world to understand itself in a new way.

5.6   That is to say, God's imaginative transformation of the world, including such a transformation of the wrath, is offered to the world as a new way of understanding the world including its wrath. Where the margin of negotiability in the world permits it, the creatures in the wrathful situation have the opportunity to turn from their destructive course and, by bringing the concrete trajectories of their efficacious power into harmony with the new divine vision, avert the imminent wrath. In some critical situations it is highly uncertain, or even extremely doubtful, that such a margin exists, but as the King of Nineveh says, "who knows?" Where the margin of negotiability proves too narrow to avert actual disaster, because the momentum of historical efficacies for destruction cannot be reversed or sufficiently deflected, still there is room for the creatures within this doomed situation to assess the situation not *just* within its own terms as doom, but from the perspective of the transcendent divine aim, an aim which transcends the doom through the transformed character of that aim. In such situations the doom is not the end, but has the character of a time of tribulation (biblical ṣārâ or *thlipsis*) and of travail, on the way to an end which lies beyond these turbulent immediacies. This tribulation can only, then, be undergone and suffered in hope, both by human beings and by God.

5.7   Two more points may be made, by way of a general understanding of the divine transforming action as displaying God's sovereign *freedom* and *power*. In a process view, the sovereign *power* of God is displayed not as an instance of unilateral and independent action (*pace* Wolff), but as an instance of relational action, displaying both passional and active aspects. It is as such that we may understand the divine life to be the eminent exemplification of "Power as the Capacity to Sustain a Relationship" (Loomer: 1976b). But what of the sovereign *freedom* so displayed? According to Wolff and Mays, as well as other commentators, God's freedom is displayed in the choice by which the divine life denies or displaces its wrath in favor of its love. But action which *divides* the self by actualizing the potential of only some of the passionate impulses, is not a display of freedom but of compulsive behavior. In Tillich's words (1957:42–43),

> freedom is the possibliity of a total and centered act of the personality, an act in which all the drives and influences which constitute the destiny of man are brought into the centered unity of a decision. None of these drives compels the decision in isolation.

If these words properly describe freedom/16/, one should hesitate to take Hos 11:8–11 as demonstrating that Yahweh's actions arise out of some one element in the divine life at the expense of another. But it may be questioned whether the text *does* this. Indeed, at this point we may appreciate how the text in fact refuses to attribute the transformation to any one discrete aspect of Yahweh, but rather simply indicates that it takes place in the divine life. In this way, the text preserves the mystery of the divine freedom of action, even as it vividly asserts that the transformation takes place. Here the significance of the idiom *nehpak 'ālay libbî* perhaps come fully into view. As suggested above, the peculiar force of the preposition here demonstrates that the action is something conceived as at the same time happening *to* the agent, so that the agent is in some sense the outcome of its own action. All this may be understood in a process perspective through the following remarks of Bernard Loomer (1976a:326):

> The self in its freedom, in its self-creation, is its uniqueness and its mystery. The self in its freedom cannot be reduced to its conditioning causes. Its decision is not simply a function of its motives, however vital they are in the constitution of the self. The choice of the self cannot be explained. The decision cannot be rationalized. The individual cannot tell another, finally, why he made the decision he did because he *is* that choice, that decision. In answer to the question as to why he made the choice that he did the individual can only reply that he is the person who made that choice. If he could "explain" his decision, he would be a function of his explanation or his motives. He would also have lost his selfhood and his own mysteriousness.

6.   Theological Overtones of Hosea 11

6.1   With the perspective gained through the above general discussion, let us now attend once more to Hos 11:8–9 and its sequel in 11:10–11. Verse 8, lines 1–4, portrays Yahweh as confronted with a genuine impasse. The wrath which arises in and from Israel's situation and which becomes the concrete existential form of the wrath of Yahweh, in and of itself has as a projected result the final destruction of the people and thereby the final termination of the Yahweh-Israel relation. This is intolerable to Yahweh. But the wrath inherent in the situation cannot simply be rejected if Yahweh is to continue to be God of heaven *and* of earth. The wrath must be drawn into the power of the divine decision, into what Buber calls the transmuting fire ("my change of mind grows fervent altogether") wherein the future is adequately forged. In a process which is veiled from our view within the mystery of the divine freedom, God's heart—God's complete affective, cognitive, puposive self—displays a transformation which pervades the totality of the divine life. The outcome is that, whereas the *initial* form of the divine feeling with its wrath would have been a departure, a turning, from Yahweh's aims for Israel, the *transformed* divine aim ensures that Yahweh "will not *turn* to destroy Ephraim"/17/.

6.2   It is in this divine act which eminently and perfectly exemplifies the true character of *yiḥud*, of existential decision toward holistic becoming, that the emphatic contrast emerges which distinguishes God as the Holy One from humankind. Whereas human beings in their finitude and brokenness constantly fall short of, and miss the mark of, such decisions and such becoming, God achieves it imaginatively within the divine life. By virtue of the fact that this Holy One is in the midst of humankind, the divine imaginative *yiḥud* becomes also the task of human beings. The imaginative unification takes place first of all within the divine life itself, within that *sōd* of *Yahweh* which is God's own privy solitariness where no one is counsellor. But the prophet, by virtue of the prophetic calling, becomes privy to the divine *sōd*; and by the announcement of the message received in this intimate context—in this instance, by the announcement of Hos 11:8–11 to the people—the whole people is drawn into the *sōd*, the inner council.

6.3   This last sentence leads us into a concluding heuristic speculation on the character and function of the sort of eschatological language which appears in Hosea. As 2:14–15 (EVV) already shows, the new future beyond judgment is portrayed largely in the terms which characterized the old relationship: new wilderness, new entry into the land, new covenant. (Note the terms in which the last feature is expressed: "and there she shall *answer* as in the days of her youth, / as at the time when she came out of the land of Egypt." The eschatological covenant, like the original covenant, will arise through the posing of an existential question to Israel, and will be concluded through a lived response which will be Israel's answer.) So also, 11:10–11 portrays a future which in part resembles the past: it will be a deliverance from Egypt (and, this time, Assyria); and it will be effected under the aegis of Yahweh the divine warrior, in the image of a roaring lion/18/. This tendency to depict a saving future by the use of images which have arisen as characterizations of the past comes to its most comprehensive biblical expression, of course, in Second Isaiah. The significance of this type of portrayal may be indicated, in the perspective of this paper, as follows.

6.4   First, the divine portrayal of the future is not merely an accommodation of the divine omniscience concerning a totally determinate future to the limitations of human powers of envisagement. For the future is not envisaged in its precise details even by God, but is entertained, even in the divine life, in the form of the directional and inclusive Eros. It is this indeterminateness of eschatological vision which provides the arena of freedom within which both God and humankind may share in the "power of fate-deciding." But this means that the eschatological images and metaphors function as symbols for God as well as for humankind. But secondly, the resemblances between past and future give assurance of the fundamental faithfulness with which the new aims of Yahweh further the original purposes shared with Israel under the old covenant. In this way there is disclosed "the passion of purpose that will not surrender in spite of frustration and rejection" (Mays:119). That is to say, the possibilities which had once become a live question for Israel, but which now threaten to become a dead issue, by the announcement of Hos 11:1–11 once again become an open question. In this question lies the fount of freedom and power by which Israel may eventually, turn and "go after Yahweh" (11:10).

6.5   Thus it is seen that eschatological existence for Yahweh and Israel is existence within the sphere of power of the deepest and most comprehensive of existential questions. Perhaps the most painful and searching of specific questions to arise within the sphere of eschatological existence, is the cry which, we may now say, arises *on both sides* of the relationship: "How long?" That question is neither a request for information nor a rhetorical outpouring of futile feeling or useless passion. Rather, a life which is lived in the power even of such a specific question is a life which remains open to the envisaged future, and which keeps itself open to the "answer" which the other party may yet give through existential decision. Thereby, the eschaton may be said to be believed *in*, even where the belief takes the form of questions which also give voice to dark and poignant doubt. If the eschaton proves to be more than its images were capable of showing, that is because each party was "saying as you go more than you even hoped you were going to be able to say, and coming with surprise to an end that you foreknew only with some sort of emotion" (Robert Frost, in Cox and Lathem:46). Which is to say that, for Yahweh and for Israel, eschatological existence is existence in faith—or perhaps one should say faithfulness, *'ĕmûnâ*—a faith or a faithfulness into the sphere of power of which, even while being subjected to other wrathful forces, Ephraim is already being invited by the disclosure of the divine word in and through Hosea 11.

NOTES

/1/ "No amount of drilled-in rules or reflexes can prepare the swordsman for the infinity of different attacks which he may have to face. . . . He is taught, therefore, never to make any specific preparation for attack nor to expect it from any particular direction. . . . He must be able to spring immediately from a relaxed center of rest to the direction required" (Watts:86). James Dickey advocates a similar approach to poetry: ". . . our encounter with any poetry . . . requires that we rid ourselves of preconceptions and achieve, if we can, a way of reading an established poet as though we had never heard of him and were opening his book for the first time. It requires that we approach him with all our senses open, our intelligence in acute readiness, our critical sense in check but alert for the slightest nuance of falsity, our truth-sensitive needle—the device that measures what the poet says against what we know from having lived it—at its most delicate, and our sense of the poet's 'place,' as determined by commentary, textbook, and literary fashion, drugged, asleep, or temporarily dead. Like most ideal conditions, this one cannot be fully attained. But it is certainly true that an approximation of such a state is both an advantage and a condition productive of unexpected discoveries in reading poets we thought we knew" (xi). Is it naive to suppose that Dickey's approach to poetry is relevant to serious biblical hermeneutics?

/2/ In view of distinct resistance in some quarters of biblical scholarship to the use of philosophical perspectives in interpretive work—in this instance the use of process perspectives—it may not be redundant to repeat what often is acknowledged in theory but then almost as often forgotten in practice: Even those interpreters who pride themselves in bringing themselves to the biblical text as philosophical virgins, in fact already through participation in the common western tradition have been impregnated with the sort of philosophical convictions which Mauser outlines. At this stage in western history, the option is only whether we shall be witting or unwitting—wise or foolish virgins—in the philosophical dimension of our interpretive work.

/3/ The Massoretic Text (similarly, English translations) has Abraham standing before Yahweh. This is by deliberate scribal alteration from an earlier form in which the text had Yahweh standing before Abraham.

/4/ In the definitive divine self-disclosure in Exod 34:6-7, the divine wrath enjoys the same essential status as the divine steadfast love, even if the two characteristics of the divine relation to humankind may be qualified differently as "slow" and "abounding." Note also the expression in Ps 95:11, a verse that is inaccurately translated as "Therefore I swore in my anger"—as though Yahweh swore in the heat of a momentary and transient state. An examination of all occurrences of the verb "to swear" followed by the preposition b- shows that what is sworn by is not something transient or inessential, but rather (as we might expect in an oath formula) by something enduring. When Yahweh swears, it is by the divine *name*, by the divine *nepeš*, or the divine glory, holiness, or self. According to Ps 95:11, then, Yahweh swears *by* the divine wrath, that is, by this constant and essential aspect of God's own being. Wolff's reading of Hos 5:10 ("upon them I will pour out my wrath like water") will not wash. The imagery of "pouring out" no more indicates the instrumentality of the wrath than does the "pouring out" of the soul (Ps 42:5) indicate the instrumentality of the latter.

/5/ In Jer 31:13, the statement "I will turn their mourning into joy" is followed by the verb *niḥamtîm* (cognate to *niḥûmîm* in the last line in Hos 11:8), which is usually translated "and I will comfort them." This translation does not really bring out the force of this verb, which basically "describes a change of mind or heart, either in an intransitive sense [where it means 'to repent, change one's own mind concerning something'] . . . or transitive 'to comfort' [i.e., to change someone else's mind]" (Speiser:51). The true force of the verb is to be seen in the internal change effected in the attitudes of the people: mourning to joy, gladness for sorrow. The synonymity of the verbs *hāpak* and *niḥam* in this verse in Jeremiah is paralleled, I will suggest, in the forms *nehpak*//*niḥûmîm* in Hos 11:8.

/6/ Rudolph translates the line "verwandelt ist in mir mein Herz," in which the verb has reference to change by transformation or transmutation. On the preposition he writes, "'1 hier nicht 'gegen' (Wolff), sondern Ausdruck 'bei leidenschaftlich erregten Stimmungen' (GB sub '*1* Nr. Iac)" (208, 212).

/7/ The word *niḥûm* occurs only three times in the Hebrew Bible. In its other two occurrences it is commonly translated "comfort," but the context suggests that "comfort" is not quite the force of the word (see note 5 above). A brief examination of the two occurrences will perhaps make this clear. Isa 57:18 reads ". . . I will requite him with *comfort*, creating for his mourners the fruit of the lips." As the following clause indicates (and in parallel with Jer 31:13), *niḥûmîm* here indicates that Yahweh will bring about a *change* in the basic felt attitude of the one referred to. The same force inheres in the occurrence in Zech 1:13. The context makes this clear: (1) The angel of Yahweh utters a lament: "O Yahweh of hosts, how long wilt thou have no mercy . . . ?" (2) Yahweh answers gracious and comforting (*niḥûmîm*) words to the angel. (3) The angel no longer laments to God, but now turns to the prophet and instructs him to "Cry out, Thus says Yahweh of hosts: I am exceedingly jealous for Jerusalem and for Zion." The very change in the felt attitude of the angel, from lament to cry of hope, illustrates what is referred to in Jer 31:13 and Isa 57:18. To sum up, it appears that in two instances, *niḥûmîm* can indicate "change of mind" in a transitive sense. In Hos 11:8, I maintain, it indicates such a meaning intransitively.

/8/ Recent discussion of the root *yḥd* may be traced in Talmon, deMoor, and Maier.

/9/ I am not persuaded by Talmon's attempt to establish a wide-spread occurrence of *yḥd* as a noun in the OT, nor by his attempt to establish for it a technical meaning "to enter into a covenant." Nevertheless, his discussion does show the natural affinity between the basic meaning of this root and the basic notion in covenanting as a binding together for future purposes.

/10/ In 1 Chr 12:17, it may be suggested that "if you have come to me *lěšālôm* . . . I will be toward you *lēbāb lěyaḥad*" describes a situation in which two parties to an agreement are to enter into it wholeheartedly, and without deceit or hidden intent to betray (see the second half of the verse). The genuine unity of such an agreement thus depends upon the genuine unity within each party for the agreement.

/11/ It is a commonplace of contemporary psychological understanding, that refusal to accept and "own" the negative aspects of one's own experience results in internal splits and dissociations which, among other effects, diminish the resulting width and intensity, and general richness and vitality, of one's sense of life.

/12/ On the human task of *yiḥud*, see further, e.g., Buber (1960a:133–35). On what grounds, one may ask, does he repudiate such a task for God? In the first passage quoted above, Buber writes in part, "Man is bidden (Deuteronomy 6, 5): 'Love the Lord with all thine heart,' and that means, with thy two united urges." Now, the language which in the Shema is used (according to Buber's exegesis) to describe the human task of *yiḥud*, in Jer 32:37–41 is used to describe something that Yahweh is doing or about to do. It is to be noted that the passage in Jeremiah is heavily Deuteronomistic in language and conceptuality, so that we are justified in comparing it closely with the Shema. In 32:37 Yahweh is shown announcing that their fate at the hands of the divine wrath (sic) is to be reversed. Verse 38 characterizes the ensuing divine-human relationship in old covenantal terms. Then, strikingly, the following verses deploy language in exactly symmetrical ways:

39. I will give them *one heart* and *one way*
40. that I will not *turn away* from doing good to them
40. that they may not *turn* from me
41. I will plant them . . . with *all my heart* and *all my soul*

Surely the language in v 41 is to be read as parallel to the language in v 39, to the effect that Yahweh's action does not proceed from a divided but from a unified intention.

/13/ For an attempt to develop a process understanding of, among other things, the wrath of God, see Janzen (1975). In that paper, it may be noted, I depart from the sort of process view exemplified by Lewis Ford (1978) in which God's power is understood to be entirely persuasive and to be completely devoid of coerciveness. In my view, the attempt to interpret the biblical tradition in terms of a solely persuasive conception of the power of God moves in the direction of Marcionism.

/14/ For a suggestive discussion of the "warm, passionate" power of the past, and the "cool" power of the future, which when disengaged from one another and from the power of transformation become demonic as *Lucifer* and *Ahriman*, see Barfield (especially 56–61 and 96–103). It is not without interest that Buber's discussion in *Good and Evil*, when it moves from exegetical reflection on biblical passages to constructive reflection on the nature of decision, likewise takes up the ancient myth of Ahriman (99–113).

/15/ See Janzen (1975:389–90), especially these lines: "In this sense only is God 'subversive' of the world as settled: 'he clothes' it with the translucency of his novel aims. . . . The past world is conveyed by God into the present finite occasion without physical 'refraction,' but clothed with the slightest and yet most enticing capacity to produce a refraction at the mental poles of inheriting finite occasions."

/16/ I recognize that in applying to God these words of Tillich about freedom, I am using them in a way which goes against his express intent. Elsewhere he writes, "Only he who has freedom has a destiny. Things have no destiny because they have no freedom. God has no destiny because he *is* freedom" (1951:185; italics in the original). Tillich here perpetuates the mind/matter split to which Descartes gave such impetus. According to the OT *locus classicus* for our understanding of God (Exod 3:1–15), however, it is not solely "Yahweh," but "Yahweh, the god of the fathers, the god of Abraham and of Isaac and of Jacob" which is the name and the memorial of Israel's God. On the latter name as suggesting the applicability of both categories of freedom and destiny to God, see further Janzen (1979, 1980).

/17/ The verb *šûb* in this line is commonly translated adverbially, as the syntax and the usage of this verb elsewhere certainly will allow. But the context of the whole passage (and indeed of the whole book), with its preoccupation with defection from covenanted purpose, suggests that the verb here refers to a possible (but negated) divine defection from covenanted purpose. Though Wolff and Mays both adopt "again" in their translations, in their commentary they implicitly follow the other interpretation: "Yahweh will not turn from his election of 'my son' and destroy the Ephraim creation by his saving acts" (Mays:157); "*šûb* denotes . . . not only the repetition of an action, but also the restoration of previous conditions, or the nullification of a deed" (Wolff:202).

/18/ Verse 10 is often held to be secondary to the chapter (e.g., Wolff and Mays). The main objections are succinctly stated by Mays: (1) the style of divine saying of vv 1–9 and v 11 (divine first person) is dropped for the style of a report with Yahweh in the third person; (2) Hosea elsewhere uses a different word for Yahweh as lion; and (3) elsewhere Yahweh as lion depicts ravaging wrath. In my judgment these considerations are not convincing, and confront other indications of the verse's place in the passage: (1) Since this verse begins the depiction of an event in the indeterminate future, and so away from the present, the shift to third person is not unnatural. Moreover, as Wolff notes in his introduction, the shift from first-person to third-person divine reference occurs in Hosea no less than fifteen times in undisputed contexts! Compare also, for example, Jer 2:2–3. (2) Since Hosea elsewhere uses a (different) word for Yahweh as lion only *twice* (5:4 and 13:7), it can hardly be insisted that he displays a pronouncedly characteristic usage from which the present instance would be a peculiar departure. Are synonymous terms and expressions not allowable? (3) It will hardly do to rule out this verse because elsewhere in Hosea the lion figure connotes wrath. The difference in connotation of the lion figure is a function of the difference in general *context*: the other two instances occur in contexts where judgment is being announced; the present instance occurs in a context where hope is being announced. One might go so far as to say that the use of the lion figure in this transformed way is an effective way of portraying that the wrath of Yahweh is now past and that the same Yahweh who was wrathful in judgment is now a source of hope. (Note, similarly, how in 2:15EVV, the same *place* which once was known as "Vale of Achor" is to be known as "Door of Hope.") (4) It may further be suggested that, in addition to the affinities of v 10 with v 11, v 10 picks up a motif which runs through vv 1–7 and rings a nice change on it. Verse 1 says that they *went* from Yahweh (the verb is *hālak*) to sacrifice to the Baals. Thereafter, the familiar Hoseanic theme, of Israel's refusal to turn back to Yahweh, is reiterated. Now in v 10 that turning back to the future is described by means of the same verb as was used in v 2 to describe the defection: they shall *go* (*hālak*) after Yahweh. In this description, the momentary movement from first person to third person divine reference serves, by the use of the name Yahweh, to emphasize that there will be no ambiguity in their future allegiance. It will not be to a "lord" (*ba'al*) whose identity is ambiguous (cp. 2:16–17EVV), but to one who unmistakably is *Yahweh*.

WORKS CONSULTED

Barfield, Owen
 1965   *Unancestral Voice*. Middletown, CT: Wesleyan University.

Brown, Francis, Driver, Samuel Rolles, and Briggs, Charles A.
 1957   *A Hebrew and English Lexicon of the Old Testament*. Oxford: Clarendon. (BDB).

Buber, Martin
 1953   *Good and Evil*. New York: Scribners.
 1960a   *The Origin and Meaning of Hasidism*. New York: Horizon.
 1960b   *The Prophetic Faith*. New York: Harper and Brothers.
 1966   *Hasidism and Modern Man*. Ed. and trans. Maurice Friedman. New York: Harper and Row.

Cox, Hyde, and Lathem, Edward Connery, eds.
 1966   *Selected Prose of Robert Frost*. New York: Holt, Rinehart and Winston.

deMoor, J.C.
 1957   "Lexical Remarks Concerning *yaḥad* and *yaḥdāw*." VT 7:350–55.

Dickey, James
 1972   Introduction to Morton Dauwen Zabel, ed., *Selected Poems of Edwin Arlington Robinson*. New York: Collier Books.

Ford, Lewis
    1978   *The Lure of God: A Biblical Background for Process Theism.* Philadelphia: Fortress.

James, William
    1956   *The Will to Believe, and Other Essays in Popular Philosophy.* New York: Dover.

Janzen, J. Gerald
    1975   "Modes of Power and the Divine Relativity." *Encounter* 36:379–406.
    1979   "What's in a Name? 'Yahweh' in Exodus 3 and the Wider Biblical Context." *Int* 33:227–239.
    1980   "Bernard Meland as Yahwistic Theologian of Culture." *JR* 60:391–410.

Lathem, Edward Connery
    1967   *Interviews with Robert Frost.* New York: Holt, Rinehart, and Winston.

Loomer, Bernard M.
    1976a   "Dimensions of Freedom." Pp. 323–39 in *Religious Experience and Process Theology.* Eds. Harry James Cargas and Bernard Lee. New York: Paulist.
    1976b   "Two Conceptions of Power." *Process Studies* 6:5–32.

Maier, J.
    1960   "Zum Begriff *yḥd* in den Texten von Qumran." *ZAW* 72 (n.f. 31):148–66.

Mauser, Ulrich
    1970   "Image of God and Incarnation." *Int* 24:336–56.

Mays, James Luther
    1969   *Hosea: A Commentary.* Old Testament Library. Philadelphia: Westminster.

Rilke, Rainer Maria
    1962   *Letters to a Young Poet.* Trans. M. D. Herter Norton. New York: Norton.

Rudolph, Wilhelm
    1966   *Hosea.* KAT 13/1. Gütersloh: Mohn.

Speiser, Ephraim A.
    1964   *Genesis.* AB. Garden City, NY: Doubleday.

Talmon, Shemaryahu
    1953   "The Sectarian *yḥd*—A Biblical Noun." *VT* 3:133–40.

Tillich, Paul
    1951   *Systematic Theology. I: Reason and Revelation, Being and God.* Chicago: University of Chicago.
    1957   *Systematic Theology. II: Existence and the Christ.* Chicago: University of Chicago.

Ward, James M.
    1969   "The Message of the Prophet Hosea." *Int* 23:387–407.

Watts, Alan W.
    1970   *Nature, Man and Woman.* New York: Vintage Books.

Whitehead, Alfred North
    1967   *Adventures of Ideas.* New York: The Free Press.

Wolff, Hans Walter
1974 *Hosea: A Commentary on the Book of the Prophet Hosea.* Hermeneia. Trans. Gary Stansell. Philadelphia: Fortress.

RESPONSE TO JANZEN:
"METAPHOR AND REALITY IN HOSEA 11"

James Luther Mays
Union Theological Seminary in Virginia

ABSTRACT

Gerald Janzen's proposed translation of Hos 11:8b has required me to reconsider my own proposal, for he has rightly seen that the verse does not involve a "turning against oneself" on the part of God. But Janzen goes too far in claiming that Hosea speaks of a transformation of God's existence; the verse speaks of the complete arousal of God's compassion. This translation better fits the context. Janzen's interpretive perspective loses sight of the determinate aspects of the divine nature. His process perspective, informative as it is, is less adequate than the view of Karl Barth which holds in better balance the tension between God as immutable and God as mobile.

0.0   Gerald Janzen's work has, by its consistent richness and range, always provoked me to a kind of thinking and learning for which I have been grateful. Certainly, this paper lacks nothing in richness and range.

0.1   This response is addressed to four issues in the paper: first, the problem of understanding the Hebrew text of Hosea 11:8b; second, the sense of v 8b in its context and the function of the questions asked by God; third, the relation between wrath and love in the divine life; fourth, the claim that theology done in a process perspective makes for a more appropriate reading of the Old Testament. These are the questions which, I think, need discussion; they omit many dimensions of the paper for which I simply record my appreciation.

I

1.1   In Janzen's judgment, the translations of 11:8b in the commentaries on Hosea in *Hermeneia* (Wolff) and the *Old Testament Library* (Mays) are forced and do not follow the most natural meaning of the text (§4.4).

Wolff translates the first measure of the line "Mein Herz kehrt sich gegen mich" (the German original) and Mays similarly "My heart has turned itself against me." At issue in these translations is the understanding of *hāpak 'al* as "turn against." Janzen objects to "indicating a polemical relationship between 'my heart' on the one hand and 'me' on the other, with the heart the victor" (§4.5). Janzen takes *hāpak* in its frequent sense of "change" and the preposition *'al* as "used idiomatically to give pathos to the expression of an emotion, by emphasizing the person who is its subject, and who, as it were, feels it acting *upon* him" (BDB:753). His translation: "My heart changes itself upon me" (§4.7).

1.2 A fresh look at the text and the available analogies shows that the semantic direction Janzen has taken is the better one, but a question can be raised about its implications. I agree that in 11:8 the verb means "change," but doubt that it means "transform" in the sense that term is used in the body of the paper. The syntactical pattern is this: a niphal reflexive of *hpk* with an aspect (organ of consciousness) of a person as subject plus *'al* with the person as suffix.

1.3 Of the seven texts listed as analogies, six do not fit this pattern. Five (Lev 13:55; Jer 13:23; 31:13; Ps 105:25; 1 Sam 10:9) are cases of *qal* transitives with the accusative of what was changed. Two of them (Jer 31:13; Ps 105:25) include *l* with what the accusative is changed into, and one (1 Sam 10:9) *l* with one changed. 1 Sam 10:6 is a niphal passive with *l* of what the subject is changed to. 1 Sam 4:19, however, does have the pattern of Hos 11:8: a niphal reflexive with an aspect of a person as subject plus *'al* with the person as suffix. The sentence describes the onset of labor pains for the wife of Phinehas when she heard the ark had been captured; literally "her pangs (*sîrîm*) turned themselves upon her," meaning "her labor came upon her suddenly, unexpectedly" (Driver:49). There is another case of the niphal reflexive in this pattern in Dan 10:16. The subject is also *sîrîm*: Daniel says that because of his vision, "my pangs have turned themselves upon me," i.e., trembling anguish came over him suddenly. No other precise analogies seem to exist, but there are two other texts which appear pertinent because they are cases of niphal reflexives with "heart" as subject, namely Lam 1:20 and Exod 14:5. Lam 1:20, instead of *l*, has *b^eqereb* with the suffix of the person: "my heart turns itself within me." The sentence is one in a sequence which describes the experience of remorse at having invoked the wrath of God. Exod 14:5 lacks any prepositional phrase of self-reference: "Pharoah's heart turned itself in relation to the people, Israel," i.e., he changed his mind after he had let them go. Neh 5:7, cited by Janzen in connection with *'al*, does have the pattern, however, with the niphal of *mālak*; Nehemiah, angered at the oppression of some of his countrymen by others, reports, "I took counsel with myself," i.e., carefully considered what to do.

1.4   All the useful analogies do describe a decisive change of feeling or of mind. But it would be forcing any of the analogies to say that the change of the person involved is "a transformation of their existence." None of them are equivalent in this respect to 1 Sam 10:6, 9 where Samuel tells Saul that he will be *turned into* another man, and the narrative reports that God *gave* him another heart.

1.5   I think a reservation can also be placed against the inference drawn from the adverb *yaḥad* in the second measure of 11:8b. Janzen concludes that it "describes the process by which 'the many become one'" (§4.9), and so to speak of a new unity of the components of the divine life (§4.10). Ultimately, the conclusion is drawn that the wrath and love of God are unified to produce a new level of existence, though the subject here is simply the plural *niḥūmīm*. Would it not be more natural to understand *yaḥad* as an equivalent of *kōl*, with which it is at times set in parallel (e.g., Ps 33:15). It qualifies a plural verb and subject with the sense of *"all together, wholly, completely"* (Cf. Isa 27:4; 44:11; Ps 40:15; 62:10; 74:6; 14:10; Job 34:15; 38:7; etc.). In Hosea 11:8 does it not go with the plural *nikmᵉrū niḥūmay* to mean "My compassion is completely aroused"?

1.6   Aided by Janzen's critique and guided by the considerations above, I would now translate:

> My mind has changed;
> my compassion is completely aroused.

And I understand the two measures as a synonymous parallelism. The emotions appropriate to the concern of a parent for a child take over in the divine life which in the situation involves a change of mind. This translation does not point, however, to an occasion in which the components of the divine life are unified in a new stage of becoming.

II

2.1   The immediate context of v 8b stands in coherent continuity with it. Verse 9a is an announcment of the content of the Lord's changed mind: "I will not enact my burning anger; I will not turn to destroy Ephraim." The parallel measures do not express an immutable decree. I agree that the fact that the Lord changes his mind undercuts the validity of such an idea. But the announcement, the climax of the saying, its message, is specific, determinate. Hosea must have understood this to be the course the Lord had decided to follow. God would not carry out the annihilation of Ephraim intended in the phrase "to enact my/his burning anger" (cf. 1 Sam 28:18)/1/.

2.2   The line of thought runs from the disputed four-fold question in v 8a through the account of the Lord's change of mind (v 8b) to the announcement of his decision (v 9a). The questions anticipate these two following elements. "How can I make you like Admah, treat you like Zeboiim?" are rhetorical questions. No verbal answer is expected from the hearers, and only one possible answer is contemplated. The questions are a way in which the Lord says that, faced with the consequences of enacting his burning anger, he chooses not to carry through. I agree that a response from Israel to the saying as a whole is surely sought. Perhaps hearing the record of the Lord's electing and nurturing love will turn Ephraim from its devotion to ruin, be a healing of their faithlessness (cf. 14:5). I agree that the formal nature of the questions does not cancel their effect as a style of communication. They convey no less than the passion of the Lord's predicament at having to assume the entire burden of faithfulness required to maintain his relation as father to Ephraim as child. Yet it is difficult to see how the questions can be construed as existential questions.

2.3   They do not appear in their context to be questions "to be *lived toward* in such a way that, in time, the self which one has become is the 'answer'" (§2.2). "The one who entertains an existential question cannot say precisely what it is that one is directed toward by means of the question" (§2.4), but God does say with definiteness and precision what he has decided. A rhetorical question

> . . . may contribute to the becoming of the one who receives it; but it in no way contributes anything to the one who poses it. One expects no answer to one's rhetorical question. For one already possesses, or rather already is, one's answer (§2.8).

That is precisely the situation in Hosea 11. The Lord's answer to the question he poses is an announced decision which is an expression of himself. "I will not turn to destroy Ephraim, for '*ēl* am I, not '*îš* in your midst *qādōš*."

III

3.1   In the paper's description of the transformation which takes place in the divine life, some objections are made against speaking of God's wrath as an "inconstant characteristic" because this way of thinking about the wrath of God implies that God may set aside his wrath without setting aside his divinity (§4.4).

3.2   Certainly any approach which slights or de-emphasizes the status of divine wrath within the life of God does not do justice to the claims of the Old Testament. But is it the case that "the two feelings are not upon a different basis within the divine nature" and that "to set aside wrath is as essentially problematical for Yahweh in the OT as to set aside love" (§4.4)?

3.3   At one point in the paper the description of the divine wrath seems to imply, at least to this reader, that it does have a status in the nature of God which is different from something more fundamental to his essence. The wrath of God is understood as arising "in the world in the form of mutually discordant, eccentrically-misdirected efficacious actions tending to the destruction of some region or all of the world" (§5.4). This evil direction is assimilated by God, becomes and is the wrath of God. It "arises from the world through God's own perfect conformal feeling of the world" (§5.4).

3.4   But Janzen also says that God does not "lose sight of his aboriginal divine aim within the sphere of which the relation with the world has been established and pursued" (§5.4). In the act of transformation which occurs, "the disparate ingredients in the divine wrath are incorporated into a wider, deeper vision . . . to which they may ultimately contribute" (§5.4).

3.5   If I understand correctly, Janzen does not wish this aboriginal vision, this divine aim, to be understood as determinate in any sense. It is difficult for me to see how that can be congruent with Old Testament thinking. But, be that as it may, the very language of the paper itself implies that the wrath of God is on a different basis in the divine life in comparison with the aboriginal divine aim. And this would, it seems, mean that in the event described by Hosea 11:8 God is sovereign over his own "emotions."

IV

4.1   Janzen's reading of Hosea 11 is, of course, only the focus for the larger claim that the Old Testament reads more naturally and suggestively for theology when construed in a process perspective than otherwise (§3.0). A process view of things, it is said, may dispense with many traditional hermeneutical devices designed to save the biblical appearances since it provides a currency of thought and language into which we may naturally convert those Old Testament portrayals where God's passionality and mutability are either asserted or assumed.

4.2   If the only alternative were one of the rigid theologies which completely distinguish and separate God from the creation, like that, for instance, of the orthodox theologian Polanus, then one would have to agree. In this connection I must repent for having written: "Hosea's many anthropomorphisms are meant as interpretative analogies, not as essential definitions" (157), to which Janzen takes exception. I do so by quoting Karl Barth (498), whose words are very much like those of Janzen at one point:

It would be most unwise, then, to try to understand what the Bible says about God's repentance as if it were merely figurative. For what truth is denoted by the 'figure' if we are not to deny that there is an underlying truth?

4.3   I do not believe, however, that the options are so limited. It was fascinating to turn to Barth's *Church Dogmatics* and be reminded that, in the section in which he deals with what he calls "the constancy of God," so much of his language and logic is coordinate with that of Janzen. Barth himself is critical of any theology which portrays God as "immobile" and says,

> There is such a thing as a holy mutability of God. He is above all ages. But above them as their Lord, as the *basileus tōn aiōnōn* (1 Tim 1:17) and therefore as the one who—as Master and in His own way—partakes in their alteration, so that there is something corresponding to that alteration in his own essence.... Biblical thinking about God would rather submit to confusion with the grossest anthropomorphism than to confusion with this the primary denial of God. In biblical thinking God is certainly the immutable, but as the immutable He is the living God and he possesses a mobility and elasticity which is no less divine than His perseverance, and which actually and necessarily confirms the divinity of His perseverance.... (496)

4.4   The point at which I sense a crucial issue in thinking about the process approach to the Old Testament is a question about what is meant by expressions like "the direction of the divine aim," "the divine eros," "the fundamental divine existential question," "aboriginal divine purpose." I am under the impression that all these terms, which I take to be synonyms, are not thought to be subject to a specific and determinate content. If that is the case, it would create a serious problem, in my view, for using them to render the Old Testament portrayal of God. I think the Old Testament gives a basis for saying that what all these expressions refer to in the divine life *is* the specific in the creation of the world, the call of Abraham, and the covenant with Israel.

NOTE

/1/   A positive phrase, the precise equivalent of this one, is *šūb mēḥārōn 'appō* ("to turn from his burning anger"). That YHWH will or may do so is said many times (Exod 32:12; Deut 13:18; Josh 7:26; 2 Kgs 23:26; Jonah 3:9; Hos 14:5; Jer 2:35; 4:8; etc.). The phrase, interestingly enough, is at home in the literature which stands in succession to Hosea—Jeremiah, Deuteronomy, and the Deuternomistic history.

WORKS CONSULTED

Barth, Karl
1957   *Church Dogmatics*, II, 1. Trans. T. H. L. Parker *et. al.* New York: Scribners.

Brown, Francis, Samuel Rolles Driver, and Charles A. Briggs
1957   *A Hebrew and English Lexicon of the Old Testament*. Oxford: Clarendon. (BDB).

Driver, Samuel Rolles
1913   *Notes on the Hebrew Text and the Topography of the Books of Samuel*. 2nd ed. Oxford: Clarendon.

Mays, James Luther
1969   *Hosea: A Commentary*. Old Testament Library. Philadelphia: Westminster.

Wolff, Hans Walter
1965   *Dodekapropheten 1 Hosea*. 2nd ed. Biblischer Kommentar Altes Testaments, XVI.1. Neukirchen-Vluyn: Neukirchener Verlag. E. T. *Hosea: A Commentary on the Book of the Prophet Hosea*. Trans. Gary Stansell. Hermeneia. Philadelphia: Fortress, 1974.

THE WAY OF OBEDIENCE
Traditio-Historical and Hermeneutical Reflections
on the Balaam Story

George W. Coats
Lexington Theological Seminary

ABSTRACT

> Biblical interpretation can proceed without serious handicap when the subject of the interpretation is singular, unhampered by complex layers in the history of tradition or contradictory positions of major themes. The problem addressed by this paper focuses on a tradition, indeed, a pericope where contradictory layers remain unresolved. In the Balaam tradition, the central figure is represented at one point as a saint and at another point as a sinner. Form-critical and traditio-historical methods clarify the character of the text. Then reflection from two hermeneutic positions probe directions for interpreting the conflict.

1.0   The Balaam tradition captures the interest of historians, exegetes, and theologians alike at least in part because of its remarkable complexity. Balaam appears as the subject of comments and stories not only in both the Old Testament and the New, but also outside of the Bible. A sixth century Aramaic inscription, for example, refers to a prophecy of Balaam. Jacob Hoftijzer (13) observes that

> at the beginning of the prophecy, there is a sort of title which is unfortunately preserved only in part. In this Balaam is named *seer of the gods*; moreover, it is recorded that the gods appeared to him in the night. . . .

The Numbers text does not name Balaam as a seer. Yet, the imagery corresponds to the context at least documented by the opening lines of the oracles in Num 24:3–4 and 15–16. In all cases, the point in common that welds such diverse tradition into a single field is the image of a non-Israelite seer with an international reputation, famous for his ability to bless and curse with power. Moreover, it seems to be clear that the seer's skills were available for hire. Particularly associated with the power of a curse, Balaam could utter his efficacious words on behalf of whatever customer. And the results would merit the cost.

2.11   A history of the Balaam tradition in the Bible, however, casts a double image for its hero. The narrative in Numbers 22–24 qualifies as a legend because it depicts its subject as a saint (Coats:1973b). To be sure, the saint is a foreigner, held quite at a distance from the people of Israel. Yet, he speaks according to the legend in the name of Israel's God. And the narrative depicts its famous figure as a paragon of a distinctive virtue. Balaam enjoys an international reputation as one who can provide curse or blessing. In the legend, however, he makes it quite clear that he speaks only what God gives him to speak. Thus, when the king of Moab sends a delegation of elders (*ziqnê mô'āb w^eziqnê midyān*) to Balaam in order to hire him to curse Israel, he does not reject the invitation out of hand. But he also does not accept it at face value. In 22:8, the lead notice for highlighting the hero's virtue emphasizes Balaam's dependency on Yahweh. "Lodge here tonight, and I shall bring back a word for you *just as the Lord speaks to me*." When the word from Yahweh is negative, Balaam declines the invitation despite the honor and honorarium offered by Balak and sends the messengers home. Not to be discouraged by an initial rejection, Balak sends a new delegation with greater honor (*sārîm rabbîm*) and more honorarium. But Balaam's response is the same. "If Balak should give me his house filled with silver and gold, I would not be able to go beyond the command of the Lord my God to do small or great." And again Balaam invites the messengers to spend the night while he inquires of God.

2.12   This second inquiry should not be taken as a sign that Balaam wavers under the temptation of so great an honorarium. George B. Gray (330–31) makes this point clear.

> Assuming the avariciousness and insincerity of Balaam, commentators have contrived to read into these verses much that is not there; thus the reason that the second embassy is more eminent in *personnel* (v 15) and carry richer presents (v 17) is that Balak saw in Balaam's refusal an indication that he had not been offered a sufficiently high reward. This is probably enough the writer's view of *Balak's* attitude; it proves nothing with regard to Balaam's.

The inquiry suggests to the contrary that at each stage along the way Balaam shows himself completely dependent on the word of the Lord. He does not assume that the word of the Lord from yesterday will be the same for the new situation of today. He assumes rather that with each new development he must inquire of the Lord in order to hear what the word for that occasion will be. Indeed, when Balaam inquires the second time, the Word of the Lord is different. In this case, contrary to the first inquiry, God gives his permission for Balaam to accept the invitation and go. It is not Balaam's greed that leads to the decision. It is the permission of Yahweh. And as if in confirmation of Balaam's virtue, the permission speech concludes in v 20 with an admonition: "Only the word which I speak to you, that shall you do." Then the condition is repeated in v 35: "Go with the men, but only the word which I speak to you, that shall you speak." This image of Balaam and God suggests that God does not tie his creature to a single goal. To the contrary, each occasion of contact between Balaam and God offers potential for something new. God might have blessed Israel in the past. But that does not commit him to perpetual blessing. Each new occasion must be worked out in its own distinctive way.

2.13   Then, in the company of Balak, the same virtue repeats its legendary tones. In v 38, "Balaam said to Balak, 'Behold, I have come to you. Now, am I really able to speak anything? The word which God places in my mouth, that shall I speak.'" V 41 should not be taken as an indication of a plot to deceive Balak. Rather, Balaam develops his ritual in order to seek a word from God without begging the question about the character or content of the word. It might be a curse. It might be blessing. He has told Balak that he will speak whatever word God gives him. Thus, 23:1–5 depict the ritual for obtaining the word. And vv 6–10 make it clear that the word is blessing. In v 11 Balak objects to this travesty against his best plans. And the objection has the ring of comic ridicule. "What have you done to me? I hired you to curse my enemies. But behold, you have in fact blessed them." Balak knows the power of Balaam's blessing that cannot be undone. But the point of the scene is not the blessing, not the Word of God. The virtue at center stage in this legend returns in Balaam's speech in v 12: "Must I not be careful to speak that which the Lord puts into my mouth?" This obedience is the central focus of the story.

2.14   But Balaam and Balak try again. The legend does not permit conclusions that in the new effort, Balaam's faith wavers, that now he decides to pursue the honorarium rather than the honor of his word. Rather, the development of the narrative suggests that each time Balak asks, Balaam must seek the word of the Lord. On the first occasion, the word was a blessing. But now it might be a curse. After all, on the first inquiry from the messengers, God had said "no" to the invitation to go to Balak. But on the second, he said "yes." On this second venture, however, just as at the first point in the legend, Balaam does not decide for himself whether to speak a blessing or a curse. Rather, the narrative informs the audience that the Lord met Balaam and put a word into his mouth (v 16). And the word was another blessing.

2.15   In v 25 the comic image of Balak returns. He must plead with Balaam that if he cannot curse Israel, at least he should not bless them anymore. But the comic retort leads to yet another instance of the legendary virtue. In v 26: "Did I not say to you that everything which the Lord would say, that I would do?" Thus, the pair try a third time for a curse. And again it must be clear that Balaam's faith does not waver. The third effort means only that on each request Balaam seeks God's word without presuming to know the character of the word by his own means. Balak's speech in v 27 now gives credit to that virtue. "Perhaps it will be pleasing in the eyes of God and you will curse him for me from there."

2.16   24:1 changes the pattern of the legend. Now the focus is not on Balaam's faithfulness in seeking God but fully on the blessing itself. For the first time, Balaam does not perform the ritual for inquiry of God's word. Rather, he speaks the blessing directly. It is possible that this change in structure, and indeed, the change in generic emphasis, signals a later development in the history of the legend. Yet, despite the new focus in the narrative, something of the legendary emphasis remains. In 24:2, Balaam's ability to speak the blessing is attributed directly to God. And the narrative introduction to the fourth blessing makes the same point. The honorarium may be revoked. But still Balaam maintains his virtue: "Did I not tell your messengers whom you sent to me, saying, 'If Balak should give me his house full of silver and gold, I would not be able to go beyond the command of the Lord to do good or evil from my own heart; whatever the Lord says, that shall I speak'?" (24:12).

2.17   Thus, at every stage throughout the narrative, the same virtue is repeated. In a static picture, Balaam appears as the saint who can do nothing other than whatever God gives him to do. In no way does this narrative represent Balaam as a seer who struggles against God, only to have God convert his words of curse into a blessing against his will (contrast Wharton). To the contrary, his will remains constant throughout the narrative. Such a characterization typifies "legend" and marks this narrative as a classical example of the genre.

2.18   It should be clear that I use the term "legend" in a technical sense, not simply as a story with a religious theme or hero, but, in keeping with the definition by Ron Hals, as a narrative with a hero whose life exemplifies a significant virtue (166–76). I would argue, therefore, that reference to the story as "saga" is misleading. James Wharton, for example, refers to the narrative consistently as saga. But he offers no explanation of the significance of the term for the interpretation of the story. Of even more relevance for this discussion is his description of the hero (40).

> In a later form of our saga, Balaam emerges as the clear type of the prophet who waits obediently for the coming word. . . . From the beginning we know Balaam as a man aware of his utter dependence upon God's word and dedicated to absolute obedience, regardless of personal loss. . . . The narrative has suffered to the extent that the moment of suspense is almost totally missing—we know perfectly well what Balaam's word will be.

Yet, he concludes (41):

> Even the enthusiasm for the supremacy of the prophetic word did not serve to make of the Eastern diviner an Israelite 'saint,' or even a 'prophet of Israel' in the

full sense. He was and remained a representative of the evil arts who could be hired for a price to essay a curse against anyone.

Wharton then concludes that the central focus of the "saga" is the prophetic word, not the seer and his virtue. Gray makes a similar observation (318):

> It is hardly overstating the case to say that Balaam is an accident, and is not of the essence of the story. He is the instrument by which the proud opponent of Israel and Yahweh is led on to his destruction.

But Gray is willing to concede (318):

> If the question of Balaam's character be raised, the outstanding fact to be kept in view is that nothing suffices to seduce him from carrying out the will of Yahweh.

This point seems to me to be central. To interpret the story as an account of God's word or even an account of a seer whose intentions are really evil is to miss the form of the story now preserved in Numbers 22-24 in deference to the other references to Balaam. In the narrative Balaam does exemplify the person who waits obediently for the coming word, so much so that the story does lose its moment of suspense. And that is precisely the character of a legend, designed not to narrate suspense but to depict a hero in terms of a saintly virtue.

2.2   This depiction of Balaam as a saint who seeks only the command of the Lord stands in sharp contrast to the image of the culprit in 22:22-34. That a problem appears here can be demonstrated readily by comparing vv 20-21 and 22. In vv 20-21 God responds to Balaam's inquiry about going to Balak with explicit permission. "God came to Balaam by night and said to him: 'If the men come to call you, rise. Go with them!'" And the permission does not violate the character of the legend. "Only the word which I speak to you, that you shall do." Thus, v 21 reports that Balaam obeyed the command of the Lord. On the next morning, he rose (N.B. the verb *qûm* in both verses), saddled his animal and followed the princes of Moab. But v 22 contradicts this scene with an announcement that God became angry with Balaam *because he went away*. The two elements stand in sharp contradiction. In the one God sends Balaam on his way. In the other he is angry because Balaam began the trip.

2.21   How, then, should the contradiction be interpreted? It seems to me to be clear that the problem cannot be solved by reference to two different literary sources/1/. The gap highlights a shift in tradition from Balaam the saint to Balaam the sinner, and indeed a shift in genre from a legend to a fable/2/. It is thus a problem in the tradition history and not in the redaction of literary sources. The purpose of this paper is (1) to explore what insights from form criticism and tradition history might be established for interpreting this contradiction, and (2) to explore how canon criticism or a process hermeneutic might contribute to the task.

2.22   Moreover, the tradition in the fable relates to the context now supporting these verses. Balaam travels from his home to some unnamed location. But the trip is in opposition to God's intentions. And thus the angel of the Lord blocks his progress. The scene eventually wins a confession from Balaam, a confession that proves the ass to be a more efficient seer than the famous seer. One must ask what the content of the sin confessed in v 34 is. Is it Balaam's trip, or is it his maltreatment of the animal, his failure to trust the sight of the ass against his own perception? In any case, the confrontation wins a concession from Balaam to return to his home, apparently in keeping with the intention of the Lord in blocking his progress. V 35 then contradicts the fable, returning instead to the focal interest of the legend.

2.23   The fable contains tradition negative to Balaam. Unfortunately, it does not clarify the nature of the negative. In contrast to the legend, it permits at most a conclusion that Balaam embarked on a trip and that the trip was contrary to the designs of the Lord. Other allusions in the Bible, however, enlarge the character of the negative pole. Deut 23:5b–6 suggests that Balaam sold his skills to Balak specifically in order to curse Israel, specifically against the will of the Lord. "Against you he hired Balaam, the son of Beor from Petor of Aram in Mesopotamia in order to curse you. But the Lord your God was not willing to listen to Balaam. The Lord your God converted the curse into a blessing for you because the Lord your God loves you." In this case Balaam acts. And God must react in order to reverse the wrongheaded direction of Balaam. The curse becomes a blessing. The same tradition appears also in Josh 24:9–10, Neh 13:2, 2 Pet 2:15 and Jude 11. The two texts from the New Testament emphasize particularly the vice of greed as the motivation for Balaam's sin.

2.24   In addition to the tradition about Balaam as a seer who sold his skills out of greed in contrast to the will of the Lord, a seer who spoke a curse only to see his curse turned to blessing by the power of the Lord, Josh 13:22 labels Balaam a diviner (*qosēm*). Diviners exercise a practice expressly forbidden by Deut 18:10 (cf. also 2 Kgs 17:17). But of even more importance is the image of Balaam as a sinner who caused Israel to participate in an idolatrous sexual ritual. Num 31:8–16 attributes the blame for Israel's apostasy at Baal Peor to Balaam. Particularly, v 16 refers to Balaam's word (*bidbar bilʿām*) as the motivating factor in the seduction of Israel by the Midianite women. Balaam was thus the tempter who caused Israel to stumble (cf. Rev 2:14 where Balaam is responsible for Israelite apostasy rather than for a curse against the people of God). In this wing of the tradition no intervention by God converts Balaam's evil intentions into good. To the contrary, the apostasy at Baal Peor becomes a proverbial occasion of rebellion (cf. Josh 22:17). And perhaps in this context the announcement of Balaam's death as a part of Israel's victory over Midian (Num 31:8–16) can most readily be understood.

3.0   The Balaam tradition obviously embraces a wide range of perspectives. Balaam is both saint and sinner. Indeed, within the framework of one pericope, he is both saint and sinner. That diversity can be understood within the scope of the tradition's history. The lines of the oldest tradition seem to involve Balaam as a willing seer for hire, a person who apparently goes against the will of Yahweh to curse Israel only to have Yahweh convert the curse to blessing. If that is the shape of the oldest tradition, the legend would have converted the image of Balaam from its negative shape, an enemy of the Lord, to its positive saintly shape. Evidence to support this conclusion derives from the fable, with its depiction of Balaam on the way to Balak in contrast to the will of Yahweh. That scene could make no sense in a positive context. Yet, it assumes Balaam's trip and, indeed, the need to send him back home (Wharton:40). But the conclusion must nonetheless remain hypothetical.

4.0   The origin of the tradition is not, however, the most pressing question. A more urgent issue arises in the light of Brevard Childs's suggestion that canon criticism demands its hearing in any interpretation of biblical tradition (73).

> Canonical analysis focuses its attention on the final form of the text itself. It seeks neither to use the text merely as a source for other information obtained by means of an oblique reading, nor to reconstruct a history of religious development. Rather, it treats the literature in its own integrity.

This statement merits highest applause. Old Testament scholarship has entered a period of activity that addresses its subject not for the sake of ancient Near Eastern history that might be reconstructed from it, nor for the sake of a sociology of ancient Near Eastern religions, but rather for the sake of the literature itself.

4.1   One of the most important contributions of Childs's canon criticism is a clarification of procedure in achieving an adequate treatment of the literature "in its own integrity." "The canonical study of the Old Testament shares an interest in common with several of the newer literary critical methods in its concern to do justice to the integrity of the text itself apart from diachronistic reconstruction" (74). Again, the orientation is cause for genuine excitement. It is time for biblical scholars to devote as much attention to the text we actually have in hand as our predecessors devoted to hypothetical reconstructions. A synchronic evaluation of the Old Testament as literature must, then, receive the heartiest welcome. Yet, it is precisely in the description of the method as it relates to the Balaam tradition that I would raise some questions and thus reflect on some growing hesitancy in embracing canon criticism as a tool for theological evaluation.

4.11   The methodological orientation appears to me to fall into a trap by virtue of a declaration of exclusive alternatives. "The canonical approach is concerned to understand the nature of the theological shape of the text rather than to recover an original literary or aesthetic unity" (74). But does the evaluation of theological shape in the text not rest on firmer foundation if some exploration of the history that produced that shape supports it? A synchronic evaluation unsupported by a diachronic probe remains as problematic as a diachronic reconstruction uninterested in the received text. Childs objects that the diachronic methods "miss the mark and have not fully grasped the methodological issues at stake in the canonical proposal" (75). But why should the issues at stake in the canonical proposal be chosen as a methodological orientation of biblical research above the issues at stake for a form-critical or traditio-historical approach? Why can we not have both the productivity of the diachronic methods and the insight won by a careful evaluation of the canonical shape of the text?

4.12   This point appears sharply in a growing sense of competition between practitioners of the various methods. Childs lists those methods and discusses the relationship of canonical study to them, at each point implying the exclusive claims of canonical study. My point is to appeal for a complementary relationship of the methods. For example, would canonical study not need to give more serious hearing to the questions Childs notes from the form-critics: "Why should one stage in the process be accorded a special status? Were not the earlier levels of the text once regarded as canonical as well?" (76)? Childs addresses this question by affirming the theological significance of the final stage, represented as canon by the community of faith. But the problem uncovered with clarity by diachronic study remains. In what manner can canonical study deal with plurality of significance in any given canonical text? Must the canonical approach not avoid the appearance of asserting that there is only one intention in the one level of a text that carries theological significance for the community of faith? Childs observes: "Often the assumption that the theological point must be related to an original intention within a reconstructed historical context runs directly in the face of the literature's explicit statement of its function within the final form of the biblical text" (75). The point of this objection is well taken. It is methodologically a weak position to construct the theological significance of a text on a hypothetical original intention. Yet, does the statement also mask an assumption about the nature of the text under consideration? Does it suggest that any text will contain a singular, explicit, integrated statement about function? What happens when the literature reveals something less than an explicit statement of function within the final form of the text, or when it reveals more than one function?

4.121   This point can be illustrated by three methodological issues: (1) Childs recognizes the importance of text criticism for the disciplines of Old Testament study. The Masoretic text is the vehicle for the Old Testament canon. But the history of the Masoretic text involves a diachronic dimension.

What happens to the canonical shape of the received text when the text must be reconstructed? Does the canonical shape hold superiority over the reconstruction, even when it must be judged corrupt (88–89)?

4.122   (2) In the Pentateuch, some texts appear to be the product of a combination of earlier, distinct sources. The canonical orientation argues that "it is the full, combined text which has rendered a judgment on the shape of the tradition and which continues to exercise authority on the community of faith." Yet, does the position assume not only a combination but also an integration of sources into a singular, meaningful text unit? A text like the flood story seems to me so obviously the product of a combination of sources that I would question the character of the authority which the combination reveals. Does the combined text retain any other authority than that which calls for preservation of the two sources? Does the authority of the received text not embrace a plurality of text stages that has not been integrated? And if so, how can the two voices lay claim to a single canonical authority? Childs observes for example, that "when the attempt is made to treat the sources as separate theological entities, an assumption of an isolation between sources is at work which runs counter to the canonical traditioning process and which disregards the way the method was used authoritatively within a community of faith and practice" (177). But does this position not assume an integration that may not have occurred in the narrative preserved in the final form of the text? Bernhard Anderson argues for unity in the flood story (23–29). But even in the light of his argument, the double character of the narrative remains apparent.

4.123   (3) Also in the Pentateuch, tradition history reveals a similar plurality of voices. Childs's treatment of the patriarchal stories in Genesis illustrates the problem. In the canonical form of the text, the stories submit completely to the theme of God's promise (150–52; see also 132). This point is clear, for example, in Genesis 22. The unit stands now under the control of the promise as renewed in vv 15–18. Abraham's obedience serves as a foundation for reaffirming the promise. But the promise element seems clearly a secondary addition to a text that already reflected a long tradition history before it was expanded with the promise. And the tradition, before it was shaped by the promise element, now standing complete in vv 1–14, had nothing to do with the promise. The promise element has drastically reshaped the content of the tradition preserved by this text (Childs:151). In what manner, then, does the legendary form of the tradition before it was converted to a promise story influence the interpretation of the canonical shape?

4.2   The problem intensifies when a text with contradictory voices comes into consideration. In the Balaam story, a legend presents Balaam as a saint, an ideal prophet who regularly affirms the prophetic virtue of speaking only what the Lord gives him to speak. But this legend stands in contrast to all the other references to Balaam in both the Old Testament and the New Testament. Indeed, it contradicts the perspective and intention of the fable now embraced by the legend. How can that contradiction be handled by a canonical analysis if the analysis cannot resort to a diachronic probe? Must it not come to grips with at least two stages in the history of the tradition represented by the two genres, each competing with the other for status as authority and each preserved, side by side with the other, in the final form of the text?

4.3   Moreover, for the Balaam tradition, it is not possible as it would be in other texts with traditio-historical problems to suggest that the shape of the text itself resolves the problem. There is, for example, a serious problem in the history of the Passover-Unleavened Bread tradition. The two were apparently originally distinct, even to the point of preserving distinct traditions about the exodus. But it is clear that the Passover tradition gained ascendancy and repressed the tradition about a Festival of Unleavened Bread. The canonical shape of the text places the authority of Scripture on the Passover. And accordingly, Passover tradition dominates the received text, just as promise tradition now dominates the text of the partiarchial narratives. I might still ask about the canonical significance of the Unleavened Bread or the fragments of tradition about the exodus as a secret escape with spoil. Is the patriarchal tradition behind the form dominated by the promise without canonical significance? But for the Balaam story a canonical tendency is not apparent. The two genres exist side by side, neither repressed by the other. How does canonical analysis deal with that kind of contradictory plurality in the received text?

4.4   This question appears to me as an enigma. Childs obviously sees a plurality in texts and treats it with methods developed by the form-critics and historians of tradition. This point is clear from his commentary on Exodus. Yet, in the *Introduction*, his affirmation of significance "only in the final form of the biblical text in which the normative history has reached an end" (76) appears to me to be ambiguous. The final form of the text enables "the full effect of this revelatory history" to be perceived. And that point, so it seems to me, embraces a depth dimension that must be probed by diachronic methods. The method claims, however, that the final form of the text exercises a critical norm over the historical dimension. That point would be relevant if the text expresses its critical, normative role in a singular, integrated intention. Passover supersedes Unleavened Bread. But what happens when the final form of the text fails to express a single, critical norm but rather reveals a plurality of norms, some competing and even contradicting others?

4.41   One way to deal with the complexity is to argue that even though the Balaam tradition does not show such a clear tendency to adopt one stage as normative vis-à-vis the other, there is nonetheless a tendency in the tradition. The New Testament allusions to the tradition consistently show Balaam in the negative pole. Does that not suggest that at least for the Christian communith of faith, the Balaam tradition functions only as a negative model of prophet, seer, and human being? Moreover, if exegetes follow through on a history of the Balaam tradition, must they not conclude that the negative pole is clearly the dominant one, both from the perspective of the earliest levels of the tradition and obviously from the latest stages?

4.42   It would seem to me to be necessary to avoid the appearance of an argument that elements of Old Testament tradition have canonical status only when they are validated by citation in the New Testament, or even when they are in some measure consistent with the tradition of the New Testament. Wharton concludes, for example, that "we in the church ultimately receive the word of God from him who is the Word of God, and therefore its witness is incomplete until it has borne witness to him. We must expect to listen to the final witness of the New Testament if we would hear the full witness of Numbers 22–24" (42). Yet, Childs does not make this value judgment on the validity of the Old Testament text. That we receive the tradition through "*Rabbēnu*," "our master," is certainly true for the Christian. But that is not to say that the New Testament witness validates the canonical status of a tradition preserved in detail in the Old. That the New Testament apparently makes use of only the negative tradition about Balaam cannot sustain a conclusion that the positive pole has no canonical value. Thus, the enigma of the Balaam tradition remains. According to biblical tradition, Balaam was a sinner of the worst order. But also according to biblical tradition, Balaam was a saint.

4.43   The question posed to canon criticism is therefore not simply: "Why should one stage in the process be accorded a special status?" It is: "How can one stage be accorded special status when in fact that stage is in itself an unintegrated, or only relatively integrated, collection of at least two prior stages?" In what manner can canonical study deal with plurality in the canonical stage of the tradition? The critic must control methodology very carefully just at this point. The Balaam tradition is not simply analogous to the Passover-Unleavened Bread tradition. The observation that Unleavened Bread must have been a distinct and independent tradition, now repressed by the Passover, depends on a reconstruction. In my opinion, the reconstruction is convincing. Yet, the fact remains that no text sets out the Unleavened Bread festival or a tradition celebrated by it in an unambiguous fashion. There is now no text that can function as a normative witness to the community of faith about the Unleavened Bread festival. That point does not apply for the Balaam tradition. Both poles of the tradition have been preserved in a relatively complete form as normative for the community of faith. Must the exegete who asks the question about canon not reckon particularly in the Balaam tradition with a plurality of formulation?

4.5   James Sanders formulates this point with precision. "The concept of canon is located in the tension between two poles: stability and adaptability" (1976:531). Yet, in what sense is the image of Balaam as a saint the product of adaptability within the dynamics of a tradition about Balaam the sinner? Sanders argues that one crucial characteristic of the canonical process was the repetition of the tradition (1976:537). What evidence suggests that the story of Balaam as a saint was ever repeated? How did that facet of the tradition give life to the community that preserved it? The question raises issues about the character of the tradition's history. "Canonical criticism picks up with the results of tradition criticism and goes on to ask what the *function* or *authority* was of ancient tradition in the context where cited. How was it used?" (1972:xvii). Can the image of Balaam the saint have canonical status if it does not reveal evidence of repetition in subsequent generations of the community of faith?

5.0   The story of Balaam as a saint does not appear at other stages in the Balaam tradition. It is as if the story itself is alien to the major scope of the Balaam complex. Is it possible, then, to sustain an argument that the field of tradition for the legend has not been correctly identified? Is it not possible that a quite distinct tradition history accounts for the presence of the legend in Numbers 22–24? If that should be the case, then the canonical status of this story would derive from that distinct tradition process, not the one cited by the New Testament. The viability of a thesis about a distinct field in the tradition history of the Balaam legend can be tested by asking about the function of the legendary story. The thesis depends on the assertion that characteristic of the canonical process is the adaptability of a tradition

> to a number of different literary forms, adaptable to the needs of peace or the strains of war, adaptable to widely scattered communities themselves adjusting to new or strange idioms of existence but retaining a transitional identity, and adaptable to a sedentary or migratory life. (Sanders, 1976:539)

6.1   The Balaam legend is not primarily a story about blessing and cursing. Although most of the allusions to Balaam outside of the legend show the tradition's focus on Balaam's blessing, or better, on his cursing converted by God to a blessing, in the legend the focus of the tradition pinpoints Balaam's obedience. The legend does not complicate the narrative with complex issues of essentially magical quality. It is not a matter of Balaam's curse, once spoken, working out its destructive power, or even a matter of the blessing. It is a matter of Balaam's obedience. The legend poses, moreover, a critical, theological issue concerning the nature of religious obedience: Does Balaam, according to the story, have the freedom to obey or not to obey? Or does the story cast him as a puppet driven at each stage by the strings of God to do what God forces him to do? The latter is clearly the case of Josh 24:9–10 and Neh 13:2. But in the legend the former is the case. Balaam never assumes the content of God's word concerning Balak's request for a curse. But in addition, the story does not assume that Balaam has no need to make his choice about obeying the word of the Lord. Balaam is not moved as a puppet to voice his blessing. Rather, he seeks evidence from God that will facilitate his choice from one occasion to the next. Even the one scene that cuts away the ritual and moves immediately to the blessing does not assume that Balaam's choice in the matter has been denied or overridden. It is simply a scene that drops the ritual of inquiry. It may put focal emphasis on the blessing rather than on the choice. But it does not deny the narrative description of Balaam as a man who chose the direction of his deed.

6.2   I propose, then, that the traditio-historical field for this legend ought not to be limited to texts that happen to allude to Balaam as the central figure. That course produces only stages in a tradition history that cast Balaam as a sinner, coerced beyond his will to curse Israel in order to complete a preordained blessing. To the contrary, a tradition history for Balaam the saint might properly include texts that depict a tradition about obedience to God.

6.21   Several examples of narratives provide an initial contribution to the field. Genesis 22 depicts Abraham as a paragon for obedience to God (Coats:1973a). The command given Abraham by God as the content for a test of his faith cannot be dismissed as an artificial trial by virtue of the introductory verb (v 1). To the contrary, the image carrying the narrative forward captures the crises of obedience. Abraham risks the prize of his family, the *only* son whom he loves, in his act of obedience. It is possible, however, to interpret the narrative pattern about this event of obedience as amoral. Abraham shows no signs of struggle with the choice he must make/3/. He simply moves without waver to the awful task called for by the command of the Lord. Yet, the evidence of his obedience leads finally to an affirmation of his faith (v 12) and then to God's blessing (vv 16–17). The affirmation of Abraham's faith contains a definition of his relationship to God: "Now I know that you fear God ($y^e r\bar{e}'$ $'^{\mathcal{E}} l\bar{o}h\hat{i}m$)." This allusion, so it seems to me, does not qualify the legend as Elohistic. Rather, it sets the pericope into the context of a tradition about faith. To obey the commandment of God is to show "fear of God." So, the introduction to the Covenant Code, Exod 20:20, shows the fear of God to be the result of the divine test ($n\bar{a}s\bar{a}h$). And Prov 1:29 connects the fear of God with the all-important choice, rejected by the scoffer or fool.

6.22   A similar legend depicting a saint as a paragon of virtue appears as the narrative framework around the poetic dialogue in Job. The story begins (1:1) by designating the famous Job as a man of integrity (*tām*) and upright character (*yāšār*) who fears the Lord (cf. Gen 22:12). Moreover, in a series of crises Job maintains that virtue. But the story does not present Job as static, a person who by nature does what he would do as an automatic response to the event. Rather, Job must decide from crisis to crisis precisely what his response will be. The image of Satan tempting Job does not reduce the hero to a docetic puppet. To the contrary, the story (2:9) sets the choice clearly before the hero: "You still hold onto your integrity (*b^{e}tummātekā*). 'Bless' God and die." And the hero responds in integrity by affirming his loyalty to God despite the adversity of the present. He remains, therefore, an example of the obedient saint, the one who chose life rather than death. "In all of this Job did not sin with his lips" (2:10). The results of Job's obedience lead to restoration. Wealth, property, and family once again belong to this man of honor. But he defends his integrity without knowledge of the coming restoration. It is significant, then, that 42:12 describes the final restoration as a blessing (*wa'adonay bērak 'et 'ah^{a}rît 'iyyob mērē'šitô*).

6.23   Finally, in Luke 4:1–15 and parallels, the story depicts another temptation by Satan (cf. Matt 7:13–14; Mark 1:13). And in this instance, as in the story about Job, the hero resists the temptation placed before him as specific and clearly-defined choices. He chooses the way of obedience rather than the way of apostasy. And the choice leads directly to his glorification (Luke 4:15).

6.241   A negative example of an obedience legend is 1 Kings 13, a story which affirms the same virtue of obedience to the word of the Lord by the failure of the hero to honor the command (Lemke; and Crenshaw:39–46)/4/. A nameless man of God delivers an oracle of the Lord against the altar at the sanctuary in Beth'el, then validates the oracle with signs of the Lord. But the substance of the legend comes, not in the oracle or signs, but in the account of the man of God returning to his homeland. V 7 describes an invitation by the king to the man of God for a period of refreshment and a reward in the palace. But in vv 8–9, the man of God declines the invitation with an explanation about the word of the Lord requiring no food or water for the man of God while he was in Israel. The issue in the command is not the rather innocuous demand to eat no food and drink no water, but rather the call for obedience. And at this point the hero is obedient to the word of God. Yet, on the return trip, "an old prophet" met him with a conflicting word from the Lord, cancelling the requirement not to eat or drink and inviting the hero to his house for bread and water. V 18b notes explicitly that the invitation was rooted in a false oracle (*kihēš lô*). Yet, even though the moral violation lay at the feet of the old prophet, the man of God was nonetheless held responsible for his disobedience. Indeed, the irony of the legend is that the old prophet who lied about the permission of God for the man of God to eat in Israel is the one who pronounces judgment for the disobedience (vv 21-22). But the point that makes the story effective, rather than a comic portrayal of miscarriage in justice, is the choice made by the man of God. He knew the commandment of God to him. He heard the alternative from the old prophet. And he chose his fate.

6.242   A legend should, however, function as an edifying narrative, a story that emphasizes certain virtues of the hero as virtues desirable for subsequent generations. The man of God fails at just this point. He carries a commission from God to eat no bread and drink no water in Israel (cf. v 8). Yet, he succumbs to the old prophet and does precisely the thing the word of God instructed him not to do (cf. v 19). But the prophet of Beth'el also falls short of a legendary ideal, as the qualification of the prophet's oracle as a lie quite clearly shows (cf. v 18). Yet, the emphasis on the motif of obedience to God's word cannot be denied. I would suggest then, that the story should be seen as an anti-legend. The hero of the story exemplifies a negative characteristic, disobedience to God's word. And the consequences of the disobedience are painfully clear. Structural analysis of the story supports this observation. Not only are the crucial movements at the beginning of the story punctuated with references to God's word to the man of God (cf. vv 9, 16f) but also the final stages emphasize a disobedience motif at crucial movements (cf. vv 21f, 26). Significantly for the story itself the prophecy about the altar at Beth'el is somewhat incidental, coming before the real issue of the story arises (cf. vv 1-6) or after the issue has been resolved (v 32).

6.3   A parallel to this negative example might be the tale of temptation in the Garden (Gen 3:1-7). The serpent obscures the choice set before Eve and her husband. "You will not die. . . ." And the trick, like the one from the old prophet, leads to disobedience. But despite the moral violation by the tempter, the subjects of the story remain responsible for their choices. They must die. And accordingly, God sends them out of the Garden. So also in 1 Kgs 20:35-36, a prophet commands a fellow prophet to strike him. When he refused, the first prophet pronounced judgment on his colleague for disobedience to the word of God. And the culprit was accordingly killed by a lion. In each case, the focal emphasis falls on obedience or disobedience to the command of God. And in each case, the choice leads to blessing or curse.

6.4   Sanders suggests that the canonical function of a tradition lies in its adaptability to a number of different literary forms. If the tradition of Balaam the saint is properly located in a series of legends and tales about obedience, with varying figures as the central hero, would other forms of literature expand this perspective? In Joshua 24, the "little historical credo" sets the context for an admonition from Joshua to the people. The admonition begins with an appeal now familiar in the history of the tradition: "Fear the Lord ($y^e r'\hat{u}$ 'et-'$adonay$) and serve him in sincerity and faithfulness ($b^e t\bar{a}m\hat{\imath}m$ $ube'^{\mathit{æ}}met$)." To fear the Lord is to obey him, and those heroes of the faith who obeyed him demonstrated that fact clearly (see Gen 22:12). Moreover, obedience is defined in terms of exclusive commitment. "Put away the gods whom your fathers served beyond the river." But it is important to see here, as in the legends of obedience, that the act of faith does not appear to be the result of a forced decision, an election with only one candidate on the ticket. For the Balaam tradition reflected by the fable, no choice appears. Balaam has a will. But his will constantly meets the coercive revision of God. The road is blocked. The curse comes out of his mouth, but it has the form of blessing. In the legend, however, Balaam must go on each occasion to the ritual and there make his commitment. And even in the one scene where he follows no ritual but makes his blessing immediately, the same commitment underlies the event. Thus, also, in Josh 24:15, the choice is the central item in the tradition. "If you are unwilling to serve the Lord, choose ($b\bar{a}ḥar$) this day whom you will serve. . . ." In vv 16–18, the people announce their choice: ". . . therefore, we will serve the Lord, for he is our God." But Joshua repeats the alternatives. The people must confirm their choice (vv 19–20). Significantly, v 20 observes that judgment against the wrong direction is endemic to the choice. But the announcement of judgment does not function in the pericope as a threat. It is cast in an "if . . . then" structure and suggests the pattern of casuistic stipulations for judgment in the Covenant Code. But it functions here as an argument against the choice made by the people. The people should know that judgment is endemic to the choice. Thus, the result of the argument is a renewed choice for the people (v 21). The judgment may well have a threatening character: "I warn you that. . . ." But it is a character that results from the choice rather than preceding it. The choice is primary, not the result of the threat for punishment (cf. Isa 65:12; 66:3–4). The same perspective would also control the saying in Matt 7:13–14 and parallels.

6.5   This interpretation of the tradition can be tested by reference to Deuteronomy 27–28. In Deut 27:1–8, a Moses speech begins with an appeal to the people to keep the law, along with instructions for ritual preservation of the law. Vv 9–10 make the appeal a direct call for obedience. The third speech (27:11–28:68) makes the contrast between blessing and curse, obedience and disobedience, explicit. Obedience produces blessing (28:1–14). But disobedience produces curse (28:15–68). Indeed, the curse will undo the exodus (28:68). It is hard to avoid the impression that in this case the threat of judgment is a sanction guarding the decision of Israel to obey or not to obey. And moreover, the reward of God's blessing also shapes the character of the decision. If Israel decides to obey, then God's blessing will continue

(28:1-14). The element of sanction, a system of reward and punishment, cannot be denied, especially in Deuteronomy and the Deuteronomistic Historian. Yet, the important point, even for Deuteronomic theology, is that the reward or punishment does not coerce the decision of the faithful, at least not in the sense of the Balaam as a sinner tradition. The reward and punishment are rather endemic to the necessary and real choice to obey or to disobey. Rather than direct coercion, they constitute the quality of God's call for the choice.

6.51 Thus, Deuteronomy 30 sets out the choice again. Obedience will bring blessing. And indeed, the blessing has the character of religious reformation or, better, regeneration (vv 2-6):

> Return to the Lord your God, you and your children, and obey his voice in all that I command you this day with all your heart and with all your soul. Then the Lord your God will restore your fortunes and have compassion upon you. . . . And the Lord will circumcise your heart . . . , so that you will love the Lord your God with all your heart and with all your soul, that you may live.

6.52 The redemption is not, however, an event which accomplishes its goals free of obligation for the redeemed. The redeemed must then live according to the stipulations of the law. Such a stipulation should not be seen as a foundation for salvation by works of righteousness. To the contrary, it defines the character of the life of a faithful member of the community for whom the deliverance has already occurred. Moreover, the task of obedience to the law should not be seen as insurmountable. It calls rather for the people to respond obediently to the full obligation. And it assumes that that obedience can be accomplished. In Deut 30:11-14, the tradition explains:

> For this commandment which I command you this day [obedience to the voice of the Lord] is not too hard for you, neither is it far off. It is not in heaven, that you should say, 'Who will go up for us to heaven and bring it to us, that we may hear it and do it.' Neither is it beyond the sea, that you should say, 'Who will go over the sea for us and bring it to us that we may hear it and do it?' But the word is very near you; it is in your mouth and in your heart, so that you can do it.

The choice must be made. And it is quite possible to make it in obedience to the call of God.

6.53 The focus of this tradition on the choice, rather than simply on the reward or punishment, sharpens in v 15. "I have set before you this day, life and good, death and evil." The choice is moreover moral. It too is qualified by obedience (vv 16-18):

> If you obey the commandments of the Lord your God which I command you this day by loving the Lord your God, by walking in his ways, and by keeping his commandments, his statutes and his ordinances, then you shall live and multiply and the Lord your God will bless you in the land which you are entering to take possession of it. But if your heart turns away . . . , you shall perish.

V 19 repeats the tradition: "I have set before you life and death, blessing and curse. Therefore, choose life, that you and your descendants may live, loving the Lord your God, obeying his voice, and cleaving to him." And again, the results appear to be something more than mere reward for obedience. Life in the presence of God permits the warmest intimacy with him (*dābaq*; cf. Gen 2:24). That intimacy is not reward for the obedience. It is context for obedience; it makes obedience meaningful and, indeed, possible.

6.54   Yet, the specter of sanction on the choice still persists. If the righteous person could not count on the rewards of blessing endemic to the choice of obedience, would he be so willing to obey? This question, so it seems to me, is precisely the question in the legend of Job. "Does Job fear God for nothing? Have you not put a hedge about him and his house and all that he has? . . . But put forth your hand and touch all that he has, and he will curse you to your face." Thus, the promise of reward is removed from Job's decision to obey or not to obey. Moreover, Job's fate looks more like punishment than reward. Thus, his decision is explicitly without the guidelines of reward and punishment. For Job the choice is the only thing. The poetry also poses Job's painful struggle with the choice. He questions. He challenges even God himself. But at each step he remains faithful. And he does that out of moral commitment to obedience. His choice does not appear to produce blessing. It appears to produce more punishment. The epilogue then confirms the faithful character of the commitment. Job has obeyed without the promise of a blessing. And that obedience brings a new blessing (42:12).

6.60   But are there not still major problems with this final concern for blessing? Is not the good news of God's presence, so apparently at the center of his blessing, conditioned by the necessary obedience to the commandments? Does the blessing not open the Pandora's box and release the demons of magic, manipulation of the god in the box, or even simply the opportunity to purchase God's blessing by righteous works? And still, the negative must be considered. Does the tradition not threaten the faithful with curses if obedience is not forthcoming?

6.61   In order to understand the tradition, then, it is crucial to explore the character of blessing in the Old Testament, along with its opposite, cursing. Claus Westermann develops a critical and quite convincing description of blessing by drawing a distinction between two types of divine activity, both of which have been ambiguously translated by the German term, *Heil* (1–14). On the one hand God delivers his people from their bondage. The specific and concrete character of this salvation marks the event as a singular occasion of history. Moreover, in the biblical tradition, this event depends on divine initiation. No merit on the part of Israel calls the event forth. It occurs without obligation laid at the feet of Israel. But the biblical tradition knows a second type of divine action, characterized not by God's coming to deliver the people, but by his presence, qualifying already redeemed creatures as a holy community of faith. This second type of divine activity, defined by Westermann as the quality of life created by blessing, endures through the entire series of events that form the history of the community of faith. "Deliverance is experienced in events that represent God's intervention. Blessing is a continuing activity of God that is either present or not present" (4). Moreover, Westermann calls for evaluation of traditions under this interpretative distinction. The regenerative act of divine grace (Jer 31:31) belongs clearly to the first. But the second implies life enduring within the community of faith qualified by obedience to divine command. The community follows the way of faithfulness (see Ps 119:30–32). In this context the law is not a means for earning deliverance. Rather it establishes the character and form of the life under the blessing. Blessing results not as a reward for obedience previously given, nor as a carrot to tempt Israel into the proper channel; rather, it is the character and form of the life of obedience itself, a life chosen by the community or the individual within the community. The promise for blessing may function realistically as a carrot to motivate obedience. But that prospect does not alter the fact that blessing is the typical character of obedient life, one of the two alternatives set before the faithful.

6.62   The simile in Matt 7:24–27 makes the same point. A man wants to build a house. He may choose to build it on a foundation of rock. If he does, the house will stand and the man will prove himself wise. The success of his building efforts is in a sense a reward for his choice. But it is a reward endemic to the choice. Or the man may choose to build on sand. If he does, the house will fall and the man will prove himself a fool. The failure of his efforts is in a sense judgment on his foolish choice. But it is a judgment built into the choice. The choice at the center of the simile is related explicitly to obedience. "Everyone then who hears these words of mine and does them will be like a wise man." To choose life, to choose the rock, to choose blessing is to choose the way of obedience. And the details in that way are myriad. Indeed, the constantly new situations in which the decisions must be made require a constant reformulation of the manner by which obedience may be accomplished. That fact explains the necessity Israel faced constantly to reformulate the law as the shape of life in the community blessed by God. Thus, blessing is the life lived in the presence of God, characterized by obedience to his command and thus by fulfillment of the goals he formulates. Blessing in this order does not belong to the quasi-magical world from which it doubtlessly derived, a world of rewards and punishments controlled by the diviner. It functions as the design of God establishing the viability of Israel. And even more, through Israel, all nations may find viability. The law is the shape of the obedience that marks life under the blessing. But the key term in the relationship is the commitment of the creature to the way of obedience, a commitment which for the creature is not beyond his means to fulfill. It is entirely possible. He must only choose the way.

7.1   The Balaam legend would thus belong to that facet in the tradition that exemplifies blessing, not simply the blessing for Israel, but the blessing open to those who choose obedience. The Balaam fable and all other elements in the Balaam tradition reflect the opposite facet. What happens when the creature chooses the broad gate, the curse? The legends of obedience contrast with the anti-legend in 1 Kings 13. Even though the man of God does not see clearly the character of the choice placed before him, he nevertheless makes his choice. And with the choice comes his death. The broad way leads to destruction. Thus, the curse is a necessary complement to the blessing. Given Westermann's definition of blessing, would we not have now to say that curse is the character of life enduring without the presence of God? And whatever the specific character of the curse, its penalty closes the potential for blessing in the opposite choice. The character of the penalty may well be a sanction on the choice. But it points nevertheless to the reality that decision for disobedience must bring its necessary consequences. So, the man of God dies in the teeth of a lion. Adam and Eve must be expelled from the Garden. And without the Tree of Life, they too must die the death of their mortality.

7.2   Thus, it seems appropriate to define the way of obedience in the Balaam tradition as the way of blessing. Such a description involves an irony. Balaam comes to Balak in order to respond to the Israelites in the name of the Lord. That response is regularly a blessing for Israel. But in fact the story depicts blessing for Balaam. As the obedient seer who can do only what God gives him to do, Balaam himself receives the blessing of God. This point becomes explicit in the third speech, perhaps inserted into the legend as a secondary interpretation of the story. In 24:3–9, Balaam blesses Israel. And thus, he stands under the traditional blessing. "Blessed be every one who blesses you, and cursed be every one who curses you." To bless Israel in the traditional, quasi-magical way is to receive the blessing of God as the quality of God's presence for the continuation of life. And this side of the Balaam tradition stands in sharp contrast to the tradition that leads to Balaam's death (Num 31:8, 16).

8.1   Lewis Ford (1972) has also proposed a hermeneutical perspective helpful for clarifying the differences between the two poles of the Balaam tradition. According to the principles of Ford's process hermeneutic, it is essential to see God's activity in relationship to his creatures explicitly not as coercive but rather as persuasive. God does not bend his creatures to fit his will but rather seeks to persuade them toward fulfillment of various potentials. The potentials available for any given emerging occasion are limited by the configuration of the occasion's tradition from the past. But given that limitation, the creatures are free to actualize the potentials they choose. God's aim in the process is for the creature to choose the potentials with the greatest richness and intensity of experience, the widest range and highest novelty of choices. But God expresses that aim not by an act that forecloses options but by persuasion designed to "lure" the creature to the fullest realization of divine aims. Yet, the creatures do not always take up the invitation to fulfill God's aims. Therefore, God's aims must continually be adapted to the limitations of particular occasions. "God's concrete response to the world in evoking the maximum value from every situation must be constantly shifting with new circumstances and can only be fully relevant to the world insofar as it is sensitive to these contingent developments" (1972:208).

8.2   There is no doubt that Ford recognizes the coercive facet of Old Testament tradition. Divine persuasion "is at least a partially alien criterion by which to appreciate biblical traditions since their understanding of divine power is rather different" (1972:209). Indeed, given his definition of divine coercion, the alien nature of persuasion in the Balaam as a sinner tradition becomes apparent. "We may define coercion as *any restriction upon the range of real possibility which would otherwise be available*" (1978:17-18). Clearly, the tradition about Balaam that depicts the seer as opening his mouth in order to speak a curse but then has God as the manipulator who converts the curse into a blessing against Balaam's will (Deut 23:5-6) represents a picture of a god who uses coercion in order to achieve his aims for the creature.

8.3   Divine persuasion cannot function here as a criterion for appreciating or interpreting the tradition. The question is, however, whether the hermeneutical perspective of process philosophy, particularly with its conception of God's power in the world in terms of persuasion, is equally alien to the tradition about Balaam as a saint. Again, the interpretative problems loom large. If it were necessary to see the Balaam of the legend as a puppet who made no decision but simply reacted to a previous divine action, the perspective of process would be misleading. It is my contention, however, that the tradition must be interpreted in terms of a genuine moral stance. Balaam is free at each occasion of ritual with Balak to decide for obedience to God's word of blessing or for disobedience and its corresponding curse. His response to the ritual is not simply a reaction to a prescribed stimulus, with no moral involvement. It is a commitment of will. God's role in the scene does not foreclose on Balaam's genuine decision to obey or not to obey. Therefore, Balaam must seek his own way by inquiring of God at each step. And the response is not limited. It might be to refuse Balak's invitation. It might be to go. It might be to bless Israel. It might be to curse.

But it is nevertheless clear that God does play a role. Balaam inquires at each stage. And he receives the response he seeks. It seems appropriate, therefore, to interpret God's power in this relationship as the power of divine persuasion.

8.41   Yet, one major problem in the history of the tradition demands attention. Since I want to say that Balaam's obedient response to God marks a life of blessing, is not this depiction of obedience in response to God guarded by the sanction of punishment for disobedience or the reward of fertility for faithful response? In the Balaam story this issue is not paramount. Balaam does what he does without reference to a promise for divine reward for it. Balaam is thus genuinely moral in his obedience. And the consequence of the tendency is that Balaam cuts the figure of an ideally free creature, capable of responding to God's persuasion without depending on promises for reward. But what of the other texts examined in the tradition's history? Deut 30:1–3 notes explicitly that obedience to God's choice produces restoration. Again, it is necessary to admit that the sanction is a part of the tradition. God judges his creatures. And the judgment can be destructive, closing off all options for the creatures' future. In this case, God's relationship with his creatures is coercive according to Ford's definition (1978: 19). Yet, this restriction on the range of possibilities for creatures does not determine their choices of the possibilities in advance. It occurs as a necessary and ordered response to their choice. The broad gates lead to destruction. And given the free choice of the broad gate, the creatures move on their way to their fate. The fact of the tradition is that a choice once made limits the range of all future choices. It limits the aims God can place before the creature. And that limitation itself, endemic to the freedom to choose, can be anticipated as the threat or promise that qualifies the choice. Thus, while the threat or promise may in a manner restrict the range of options open to the creature, the restriction is of a different sort than the coercion in the Balaam as a sinner tradition. The restriction is a necessary boundary on freedom.

8.42   In this case, however, the threat of punishment or the promise of reward would not be understood by the biblical tradition as restricting options, but rather as quality elements in the options that influence the decision. Ford observes: "The absence of complete causal determination is a necessary but not a sufficient condition for persuasion; there must also be the evaluation of alternative possibility. For process theism, this evaluation ultimately stems from God and constitutes the way he acts in the world by divine persuasion" (1978:19). I would want to inquire, then, whether the threat of punishment or the promise for reward might function precisely as a constitutive element for an evaluation of alternatives, not as a coercive restriction of alternatives. In the Balaam as a saint tradition, process categories face no problems. In the broader range of the tradition, this judgment could also apply if threat or promise can be seen as the content of God's persuasive lure for creatures. Yet, Ford objects (1978:19):

> Such threats disturb the evaluation of future possibilities for their own sakes by attaching to these possibilities further consequences which are so undesirable as to eliminate them from serious consideration. While threats are generally most effective in restricting our options, promises of rewards may also work in this way. A possibility may no longer be judged on its own merits, but in terms of the reward it promises. In the absence of such coercive measures, however, the evaluation of real possibilities is genuinely persuasive, and influences purposively creaturely decision.

Thus, the Balaam as a saint tradition can be understood in terms of divine persuasion. Blessing for Balaam is never an issue. But the tradition in Deuteronomy, which seems to capture the same moral freedom, the same call to choose, would employ a coercive element according to Ford's categories. Perhaps here can be seen most clearly an element of biblical tradition that holds persuasive and coercive elements in tension (Coats, 1975).

9.0   It seems appropriate to me, therefore, to confirm an equation between the blessing of God in the Old Testament as Westermann has described it, a blessing that characterizes the continuity of the obedient life, a gift of God that enables the obedient creature to live within the community of faith, and the power of God described in terms of divine persuasion by Ford. God seeks his creature with his blessing, with his lure for commitment. The commitment is to obedience, obedience qualified by God's greatest aim for his creature. For Balaam, it is to say only what God gives him to say. But Balaam is always free to respond to that aim as he will.

9.1   The character of this relationship can be developed still further. The Old Testament gives form and shape to the tradition about obedience by prescribing the content of God's will in terms of commandments and laws. Thus, commandments of various sorts and content tell faithful Israelites what they should do. This dimension also recognizes that the choice placed before the creature is not simply broad gate versus narrow. It is rather a range of choices as complex and variegated as the law itself. Indeed, the history of the law shows that each generation of Israelites had to reformulate the law in the light of its own unique experience. And that law is not antithetical to God's desire to bless his creatures. In Ford's terms, it is not antithetical to God's quest to enrich his creatures' lives in any given occasion by placing before them the highest aim which they are capable of completing. Indeed, the enrichment occurs as a qualification of the initial aims placed before the creature. The law itself is a blessing, its character the enrichment of the aims God offers. "For this commandment which I command you this day is not too hard for you, neither is it far off." In this framework of life, the law is not a burden. It is an expression of blessing, a formulation of God's greatest aim for his creature (cf. Ps 119:28-32, 173-175). And in that blessing, the law would be gospel.

9.2   In what manner, then, would it ever be appropriate to see the law as a burden? Westermann makes an invaluable distinction for this tradition. The event of deliverance lies in the past. It occurred on the basis of divine initiation, totally unmerited by the creatures involved. It is thus a gift of divine grace. But the event is different from the event of blessing. God's blessing permits the moral decision. And each time the decision must be made, the blessing takes on a new tone. The law does not qualify the event of deliverance. It qualifies the life of blessing. But if the creature confuses the two and places obedience to the law as a qualification for participation in the event of deliverance, then the law becomes a burden. It interferes with the freedom of God to deliver his creatures as he chooses. Ford's categories also speak to this complex. The blessing, the power of God to persuade creatures in anticipation of their choices, is the power of the future. It is here that God's lure expresses its call for obedience to the creature. And indeed, it is here that the lure takes on the form and shape of law. If law functions as an expression of God's power to persuade, it is blessing. If it functions as a rigidifying of the power of the past, it lapses into negative form. It becomes a burden. Indeed, it becomes coercive rather than persuasive.

10.1   It would be a simple matter to conclude that the major part of the tradition history for the focus on obedience/choice belongs to the Deuteronomistic Historian. Certainly the appeal for obedience to the commandments of God is well-known as a characteristic motif in Deuteronomy. Moreover, the anti-legend in 1 Kings 13 and its parallel in 1 Kgs 20:35–36 play a significant role in Deuteronomy. But it would not be appropriate to conclude simply that the tradition itself is the creation of Deuteronomy. This point is already clear in 1 Kings 13. Lemke observes: "We do not mean to suggest, however, that a Deuteronomistic editor invented either of these themes, or that our story is simply a theological construct of his. In all likelihood, he was utilizing a pre-existing tradition that was congenial to his own purposes and which he adapted and included for reasons of his own at this particular juncture in his history" (313). It would not be correct to say, then, that the Balaam as a saint tradition is a creation of Deuteronomy, or even that it is edited by Deuteronomy. Lemke suggests a tradition history for 1 Kings 13 that would place the origin of the story in the circle of Northern prophets. Yet even for the 1 Kings 13 story, the conclusion is equivocal. "Thus while the evidence is not clear or unambiguous as one might wish, there is nothing in the first part of our story that prevents us from adopting the position arrived at on other grounds, namely that the ultimate provenance of our story is to be sought among Northern prophetic circles" (316). I do not see corresponding evidence to suggest that the Balaam as a saint tradition with its location in obedience/choice belongs necessarily to Northern prophetic circles. The literary source most likely present in the Balaam as a saint story is J, not E. But the formulation is again not simply the creation of J. It is a part of the folk theology fundamental in the formation of Israel's early tradition. Its theological contribution lies at the center of Israel's life story.

10.2   It appears to me to be clear, then, that any contemporary discussion of theology in the book of Numbers cannot choose one single canonical form of the Balaam tradition as the one with theological relevance to the exclusion of the other. If the canonical tendency in the Balaam tradition were followed to a conclusion that the Christian Church should appropriate the sinner facet and leave the saint for the Old Testament, the church would lose a significant dimension of its heritage. To the contrary, the diversity in the tradition's history points to an enrichment of the tradition characteristic for the canonical process itself. The life of obedience to God's will is not dehumanizing but rather enriching in its diversity of moral decisions. But it is precisely in that diversity that God's blessing makes its mark most effective. Canonical criticism can illumine the tradition only by making that diversity apparent and useful in the moral structure of today's communities of faith.

In contrast a process hermeneutic holds the potential for raising productive questions for uncovering a biblical theology in the Balaam story. By setting the categories of blessing-cursing into the framework of a process construction, employing the concepts of persuasion-coercion, the intention of the legend emerges. Obedience, the focus of the legend, and its corollary, the will of God that calls for obedient response, gain distinct resolution under the stamp of divine persuasion. Only in this context can the subject of obedience appear as something other than a marionette controlled by divine strings.

NOTES

/1/   Cf. Snaith (288): "This story is generally allocated to the J-tradition. . . ." This J tradition would stand in contrast to the E tradition in vv 15–20.

/2/   On legend, see Hals. On fable, see Coats (1981).

/3/   See the artistic representation of this agonizing problem in S. Kierkegaard.

/4/   Lemke's concern to establish the integral role of 1 Kings 13 in the Deuteronomistic history will be discussed in greater detail below. Crenshaw observes (43) that the purpose of the story is not likely "to teach a moral about the disobedient prophet, for the man of God is pictured favorably in the narrative, as the request by the *nabi'* to be buried beside his bones indicates." Yet, one must observe the steady emphasis in the story on the necessity for the man of God to obey the commandment not to eat during his sojourn in Israel. The crux in the structure comes precisely at the point of his disobedience. And the conclusion shows what happens to a disobedient prophet. The fact that the *nabi'* is buried next to the bones of the man of God does not detract from the emphasis of the legend on disobedience by the man of God. It shows rather that the *nabi'* is also culpable for the disobedience, a point emphasized in the body of the story by the reference to his words as lying words (v 18).

WORKS CONSULTED

Anderson, B. W.
    1978   "From Analysis to Synthesis: The Interpretation of Genesis 1:11." *JBL* 97:23–29.

Childs, Brevard
    1979   *Introduction to the Old Testament as Scripture.* Phildelphia: Fortress.

Coats, George
    1973a   "Abraham's Sacrifice of Faith. A Form-Critical Study of Genesis 22." *Int* 27:389–400.
    1973b   "Balaam: Sinner or Saint." *BR* 18:21–29.
    1975   "The God of Death. Power and Obedience in the Primeval History." *Int* 29:227–39.
    1981   "Parable, Fable, and Anecdote. Storytelling in the Succession Narrative." *Int* 35:368–82.

Crenshaw, James L.
    1971   *Prophetic Conflict. Its Effect Upon Israelite Religion.* BZAW 124. Berlin: de Gruyter.

Ford, Lewis S.
    1972   "Biblical Recital and Process Philosophy. Some Whiteheadian Suggestions for Old Testament Hermeneutics." *Int* 26:198–209.
    1978   *The Lure of God. A Biblical Background for Process Theism.* Philadelphia: Fortress.

Gray, George
    1903   *A Critical and Exegetical Commentary on Numbers.* ICC. Edinburgh: T. and T. Clark.

Hals, Ron
    1972   "Legend: A Case Study in Old Testament Form-Critical Terminology." *CBQ* 34:166–76.

Hoftijzer, Jacob
    1976   "The Prophet Balaam in a 6th Century Aramaic Inscription." *BA* 39:11–17.

Kierkegaard, S.
    1945   *Fear and Trembling. A Dialectical Lyric.* Princeton: University Press.

Lemke, Werner E.
    1976   "The Way of Obedience: 1 Kings 13 and the Structure of the Deuteronomistic History." Pp. 301–26 in *Magnalia Dei. The Mighty Acts of God. Essays on the Bible and Archaeology in Memory of G. Ernest Wright.* Eds. F. M. Cross, W. E. Lemke, P. D. Miller. New York: Doubleday.

Sanders, James
   1972   *Torah and Canon*. Philadelphia: Fortress.
   1976   "Adaptable for Life: The Nature and Function of Canon." Pp. 531-60 in *Magnalia Dei. The Mighty Acts of God. Essays on the Bible and Archaeology in Memory of G. Ernest Wright*. Eds. F. M. Cross, W. E. Lemke, P. D. Miller. New York: Doubleday.

Snaith, N. H.
   1967   *Leviticus and Numbers*. The Century Bible. London: Nelson.

Westermann, Claus
   1978   *Blessing in the Bible and the Life of the Church*. Trans. Keith Crim. Overtures to Biblical Theology. Philadelphia: Fortress.

Wharton, James A.
   1959   "The Command to Bless. An Exposition of Numbers 22:41-23:25." *Int* 13:37-54.

THE DIVINE CURSE UNDERSTOOD
IN TERMS OF PERSUASION

Lewis S. Ford
Old Dominion University

ABSTRACT

In this reflection upon Coats's essay, a background presupposition of the Balaam story comes to the fore: God has the power to discipline his servants should they become disobedient to his commands. Process theism can appropriate divine commanding in terms of persuasion, but the notion of sanctions going beyond such persuasion is highly problematic, whether in the form of outright punishment, or in notions of divine wrath, or in terms of threats. Divine cursing, however, is a possible sanction, if we allow one modification in Whitehead's theory, understanding by cursing any diminishment in the valuation God attaches to the possibilities he supplies to every emergent self.

1.1   In his use of my process categories of interpretation, George W. Coats correctly concludes, in my judgment, that they cannot be fruitfully applied to the Balaam as sinner tradition, but they can be to the other tradition. In process theism God acts by purely persuasive means, providing those aims which Balaam the saint faithfully obeys. Yet Coats asks, can process theism specify any divine sanctions which would follow if those aims were not obeyed? This feature may be in the background of this particular story, but it is a strong element in the Old Testament tradition as a whole, and one which process thought appears to neglect.

1.2   Process theism, as I understand it, seeks to conceive God purely in terms of persuasive power. All other causes may act upon us efficiently, but God is the ultimate dynamic source of final causation. Other causes are enabling or restricting causes, but God provides that ultimate lure which urges us forward. By 'persuasion' we mean that 'relational power' Bernard Loomer speaks of, a power exercised together with its recipient, in contrast to the 'coercion' of 'unilateral power,' where the activity of the recipient has no impact on the exercise of the power. Neither term is particularly biblical. Yet divine persuasion may very well describe God's activity in creation as depicted in Genesis 1. We have been accustomed to thinking of the unilateral power of divine fiat, calling the world into being *ex nihilo*, but the image here might depict the King of the Universe commanding his hosts to fashion the world by stages. Instead of repetitiously congratulating himself on the success of his omnipotent handiwork, God periodically checks up on his servants to see how well they carry out his commands: "And God saw that it was good." The image of the king commanding, which is basic to much of the Old Testament, is primarily a persuasive image. Commanding is that form of persuasion which has the backing of authority.

1.3   Yet the king has certain sanctions he can employ if his commands are not obeyed. These negativities, as they apply to the divine-human encounter, are extremely difficult to comprehend in process terms. Is it even meaningful, in these terms, to speak of divine cursing, threats, wrath, or punishment? Those process theologians who have addressed the problem (Janzen, Williams) have either treated God as the mediator of a destructive past, or have understood God to introduce additional coercive factors into the situation (Ford, 1978b:43f, notes 4, 18, 19). If God merely mediates a destructive past, then it is ultimately that past and not God which destroys us. On the other hand, it is difficult to see how any divine coercive power could be limited. It should be infinite, as befits divine power. But if infinitely exercised, it would eliminate all creaturely freedom. If its infinite power were held in abeyance, in order to allow for creaturely freedom, why then is it not used from time to time to mitigate the disatrous results of creaturely freedom? Because of these difficulties we opt for a purely persuasive power, which alone as infinite can foster creaturely freedom. Yet without coercion, how can the dark side of God be expressed? There is reason behind the summary judgment Emil Fackenheim once uttered to me in private conversation: "The process God is not stern enough."

2.1   Now if God can bless, it ought also be possible for God to curse. The author or authors of Deuteronomy 26 and 27 certainly thought so. In sending for Balaam, Balak was confident that Balaam could persuade his god to curse Israel. We hope to show how such cursing can be meaningfully understood within the limits of divine persuasion alone. Like commanding, we shall argue that cursing is a form of divine persuasion. But other terms for divine negativity are less tractable.

2.2   The notion of divine punishment, for example, has barely survived the biblical period. For the notion to be effective, there must be some sort of correlation between one's actions and one's fate. The book of Job has shown how problematic that is (Ford, 1978b:131-133). If God controlled events in detail, as the early Israelites believed, God could establish just such a correlation to reward the righteous and to punish the wicked. In the process perspective, however, the powers of this world necessarily intervene. The joint outcome of divine persuasion and creaturely realization is unpredictable, and grossly distorts the divine intention. What finally happens to people may very well be received as punishment, but whether this is *divine* punishment is harder to discern.

2.3   The image of divine wrath poses its share of problems. According to the account in Exodus, the Lord gets angry enough at Israel to seek to destroy her, and only relents as a result of Moses' vigorous intercession. Perhaps we should say that his anger cools down as a result of Moses' ministrations (Exod 32:9-14). Many find such passionate images to be crude anthropomorphisms, unworthy of deity. The psychic state appropriate to divine perfection should be pure happiness and joy, unmarred by tempermental outbursts. Furthermore, divine wrath suggests God's exclusive preoccupation with one people's misdemeanors, whereas God should be concerned about all creatures, great and small here on earth, not to mention the myriad other possible worlds in space. Instead of considering inner psychic states, which entail these difficulties, we shall concentrate on acts that result from God's negative states, such as threats and cursings.

2.4   How shall we handle the concept of divine threats? In the previous essay, Coats suggests that the threat of punishment could function as a constitutive restriction of alternatives. In *The Lure of God*, I did discuss threats as coercive, defining coercion generally as "any restriction upon the range of real possibility which would otherwise be available" (Ford, 1978b:17f). This would seem to mean that God acts coercively in making threats, contrary to my insistence from a process perspective that God acts purely persuasively. I should point out, however, that the analysis in *The Lure of God* considered threats *insofar* as they were coercive, not the whole range of threats. I had in mind such threats as a brandished pistol during a robbery, or the taking of hostages to back up one's demands. Threats range from such coercive measures to the simple indication of the consequences to which certain acts are likely to lead in the normal course of events. The latter need not be construed as coercive.

2.5   Those threats of interest to us here would be various declarations of divine intent. These declarations are the burden of much prophecy, which proclaim what God intends to do with the people if they persist in their (usually evil) ways. Insofar as these declarations are threats of punishment, then how God can make good on these threats becomes problematic, because in the economy of process theism God does not have direct control over the course of events. God's influence is always mediated by the free creaturely actualization of those possibilities God provides. What finally happens can only be ascribed to God in a highly indirect way, as the original instigator of its possibility. In terms of the classical concept of omnipotence, God's action could directly affect the outcome, in which case the threat of divine punishment could be very meaningful. The way these threats could be disregarded in practice, and the discrepancies between conduct and reward, dramatized by Job, should have suggested that something was wrong with that theory. If in its place we adopt a notion of a purely persuasive God, we shall have to abandon both the notion of divine punishment, and the meaningfulness of threats based upon divine punishment.

2.6   This need not apply to the threat of divine curse, however, because God is the direct, primary agent in blessing and cursing, whereas God's influence is highly indirect with respect to rewards and punishments. If we can establish a credible theory of divine cursing as a form of persuasion, then the threat of cursing, such as is conditionally visited upon potential transgressors in Deuteronomy 27, can be appropriated as well. Normally the curse is issued as a threat only; we are concerned with the way that curse could be carried out as a form of persuasion.

3.1   We have just seen that notions of divine punishment, and wrath, as well as the notion of divine threats, accords ill with a process perspective, but we have reserved for positive treatment the concept of divine cursing. To show how that could be possible, we must rehearse some basic features of Whitehead's metaphysics. It is primarily concerned with the process (called "concrescence") whereby actualities come into being. In that process the many causal influences from past actualities grow together (*con + crescere*) to form new actualities. The process of concrescence needs to be guided by some aim towards unity, and that aim must be received from somewhere. The aim may be mediated by other actualities, although Whitehead does not speculate about this possibility. In the end, however, God is the only ultimate source of these aims, as the ultimate source of novelty for any of the actualities of the world (Whitehead:382). Each occasion is free to modify the aim it initially receives, but it must receive some aim, including whatever novelty it could possibly achieve, from God at the outset.

3.2   Whitehead stipulates that this initial aim which God provides is the best possibility actualizable in that particular situation. Let us suggest a possible modification, however. What if, instead of automatically providing the best, God provides something less? Suppose God chooses to diminish the degree to which God favors some alternatives and disfavors others, such that the concrescing actuality experiences all the possibilities it receives from God as equally insipid? Could not this be what it means to experience the curse of God?

3.3   We propose to understand divine blessing/cursing in terms of this sort of free modulation in God's valuation of initial aims. That there could be any such modulation is contrary to standard process thought, and may not be possible in the end, when all the implications of this proposal have been worked out. In the meantime, however, it is a topic well worth exploring for its own sake.

3.4   This proposal would modify Whitehead's own theory, at least as expressed in one instance: "The initial aim is the best for that *impasse*" (373). This aim is not just a single possibility, for it "determines the initial gradations of relevance of [the possibilities] for that process of actualization" (374; cf. 46). All the different possible alternatives for that concrescing actuality have been valued by God. This is, however, only the initial valuation, subject to modification and re-evaluation by the concrescing subject (375).

3.5   Without this subsequent modification, we would have a divine determinism similar to that of Leibniz. In the *Discourse on Metaphysics* (paragraph 30), he remarks:

> Furthermore, by virtue of the decree which God has made that the will shall always seek the apparent good . . . (in regard to which this apparent good has always in it something of the reality expressing or imitating God's will), he, without necessitating our choice, determines it by that which appears most desirable.

Reasoning analogously, in a Whiteheadian context, each concrescing subject, receiving from God the best possibility for its fulfillment, would naturally remain with that one for its actualization. Why should it ever choose less than the best? On what basis could it ever make a different evaluation than that which it has received? From a *purely* rationalistic perspective, that question is unanswerable. Yet without any such modification the concrescing subject exhibits no autonomy.

3.6   At an earlier stage of his theory, when subjective unity during concrescence did not appear so problematic to him, Whitehead had a livelier sense of the subject determining its own aim during the process of actualization itself:

> Process is the growth and attainment of a final end. The progressive definition of the final end is the efficacious condition for its attainment. The determinate unity of an actual entity is bound together by the final causation towards an ideal progressively defined by its progressive relation to the determinations and indeterminations of the datum (227f).

Each subject was free gradually to define the final form it would actualize.

3.7   Later, however, Whitehead realized how problematic that notion of an initial subject must be: a subject guiding a process of actualization when neither has yet come into being! At this point he interprets subject in terms of subjective aim (342f), and settles for a theory deriving a single initial aim from God (373f; c.f. Ford, 1978a:150f). The theory of subjective aim must account for these four factors: (a) final causation, including order and valuation; (b) the possibilities for actualization, including novel possibilities; (c) subjective unity; and (d) subjective autonomy. Any theory utilizing God's provision of initial aims to explain the possibility of cursing must account for these, even if it should relax the requirement that every initial aim be the best for that concrescence.

4.1   One alternative we could consider would be to interpret cursing as the divine restriction on the range of possibilities open to a particular concrescing subject. By this I do not mean the simple withholding of novel possibilities, but the limitation of already previously realized possibilities that would otherwise be available in that situation. Since this range of possibilities is otherwise determined by the past efficient causal factors, God would here be acting coercively, not persuasively. If God could restrict the range to any degree, what principle would prevent this divine infinity from restricting it entirely? Then the concrescing subject would literally not have any alternative. Divine restriction would ultimately result in divine determinism. This would be an unacceptable alternative, in terms of both the biblical emphasis on freewill and the process concern for freedom.

4.2   On our proposal, God provides the subject with all the possibilities but withdraws all valuation from them. Suppose God chooses to diminish the degree to which he favors some alternatives and disfavors others. Then the concrescing actuality experiences all the possibilities it receives from God as equally empty and meaningless. This would be one way to experience the curse of God.

4.3   Were there already a subject present capable of receiving these unvalued alternatives, such a theory might work. But one of the functions of the initial aim, as we have seen, is to constitute just such a subject, at least initially. The initial subject *is* the feeling of that initial aim. Hence some one possibility has to be chosen as best to be singled out from all the rest.

4.4   What is chosen as best, however, need not be best in some absolute or metaphysical sense. We may be unduly restricting God's freedom of valuation by supposing that God ranks all the possibilities from best to worst according to those factors pertaining to the immediate situation. Larger considerations are also relevant. For example, at one time a concern for the evocation of intensities (Whitehead:161) would lead God to favor those possibilities for prebiotic molecules that would eventuate in living organisms, but now the invention of life makes that all unnecessary here on earth. Now, perhaps, the best possibilities for such molecules might be to remain just what they are. Stability in the inorganic realm is to be prized. In other cases, several alternatives may be equally good, though for the sake of subjective unity one must be chosen.

4.5   If God has freedom in valuing, it would seem that the prior life of the individual would be relevant to any judgment made now. Here the curse of God as punishment could take the form of a re-evaluation of the possibilities that people confront in such a way that they embrace, at least, initially, some which are objectively far worse for themselves than they might otherwise have received.

4.6   If God has such freedom in valuing, such that we do not automatically receive that which is metaphysically best in every situation, then blessing is not an automatic affair. This situation makes cursing possible, but blessing as well. Blessing, then, becomes a contingent thing, absent much of the time, but when present, something to be especially prized.

4.7   Along with valuation of possibilities goes the process of making possibilities relevant. "Apart from God, [possibilities] unrealized in the actual world would be relatively non-existent for the concrescence in question" (Whitehead:46). God is the agency of relevance. Thus, although God cannot restrict the range of possibilities ordinarily realized in a given situation, God can increase that range by introducing hitherto unrealized possibilities. In this way novelty enters the world. Creative work depends crucially upon novel insight. Perhaps in those moments the creative mind is peculiarly blessed by God.

WORKS CONSULTED

Ford, Lewis S.
    1978a   "Some Proposals Concerning the Composition of *Process and Reality.*" *Process Studies* 8:145–56.
    1978b   *The Lure of God: A Biblical Background for Process Theism.* Philadelphia: Fortress.

Janzen, J. Gerald
    1975   "Modes of Power and Divine Relativity." *Encounter* 36:379–406.

Leibniz, Gottfried Wilhelm
    1924   *Discourse on Metaphysics, Correspondence with Arnauld and Monadology.* Trans. G. R. Montgomery. Rev. ed. Chicago: Open Court.

Loomer, Bernard
    1976   "Two Conceptions of Power." *Process Studies* 6:5–32.

Whitehead, Alfred North
    1929   *Process and Reality: An Essay in Cosmology.* New York: Macmillan.

Williams, Daniel Day
    1949   *God's Grace and Man's Hope.* New York: Harper and Row.

TRAJECTORIES AND HISTORIC ROUTES

John B. Cobb, Jr.
School of Theology at Claremont

ABSTRACT

James Robinson has contributed to the conceptualization of early Christian history by his notion of trajectories. This enables us to see the multiplicity of historical movements within the church in a more orderly way. The image still fails to sustain the fully processive intentions of Robinson and could be improved by considering the Whiteheadian notion of living historic routes. This allows for both the continuity and the relative independence of the several "trajectories" and also their interactions and partial transformations through original impulses. When the element of self-transformation inherent in living historic routes is recognized, the issue of appropriate and inappropriate change must be faced. Whitehead provides assistance at this point as well.

I

1.1 Historical study withers when it is altogether separated from normative questions. It gains its importance and its direction from the judgement that its results make a difference today and tomorrow. This difference may be conceived in a variety of ways. Historians may study the past to help us better understand who and what we are or to throw light on some current problems by showing how similar problems have been dealt with in the past. Historians may intend, by bringing the past alive, to bring the present into question or to confront readers with new possibilities for their existence. They may put the present in perspective by showing that it is the result of a process which can be understood as progress and from which the direction of the future can be projected. They may present the course of events as the decay of some earlier excellence. Or they may show that the complexity of events prevents us from grasping human reality in any conceptual or imaginative scheme.

1.2 Partly because Christian scholars have felt less bound to the normative character of the Old Testament than of the New, Old Testament scholarship has freely explored a variety of ways in which history can have relevance and importance for the present. There has been less need in Old Testament scholarship to harmonize apparent diversities or to determine which of the Old Testament traditions is normative in relation to the others. Consequently Old Testament scholarship, more than New Testament scholarship, has moved toward a study of the history of traditions. Today this includes a history of the canonization process. The suggestion, often not fully articulated, is that the way in which traditions were transmitted, transformed, and selectively determined to be canonical in various times and places has some normative significance for us today.

1.3   New Testament scholarship, on the other hand, has been forced to deal more continuously and systematically with the authority of its texts. Therefore, the normative element has been particularly important in the study of the New Testament. This has sometimes inhibited scholarly integrity, but more often it has led to refinement of historical method such that New Testament scholars have given important leadership in historiography and hermeneutic. Some New Testament scholars, weary of the complexity of the problems, may prefer to consider themselves pure historians, supposing that such a category frees them from normative considerations. This enables them simply to recognize and report the confusing multiplicity of the New Testament material without asking about the relative importance of its several strands. But the major contributions to the study of the New Testament have been made by those who have struggled to identify normative Christianity.

1.4   The most influential effort to identify the normative element in the New Testament since World War II has been that of Bultmann. For him what is normative is the preached Word, the *kerygma* of the primitive church. Even in the New Testament itself we can trace the declining apprehension of this Word and the process of distortion. Clearly the history of the church comes into judgement by its failure to be faithful to this Christian essence.

1.5   The tension between this identification of the Christian essence and the historical consciousness quickly expressed itself even among Bultmann's pupils. It is particularly apparent in the new quest of the historical Jesus. Those who have pursued this quest have believed that the *kerygma* of the earliest believers was grounded in the Jesus whose death and resurrection they proclaimed. To abstract it from this ground was unhistorical. In the case of Ebeling the normative essence becomes the word-events of Jesus' own ministry.

However, the shift of the normative essence from one point to another does not deal adequately with the problem. Jesus' message is continuous with the Judaism of his time just as the *kerygma* is continuous with Jesus' message. In each case there is some originality or discontinuity, but there is also massive dependence and continuity. Further, to regard all that happens after the primitive church as at best partial faithfulness and at worse perversion (see, e.g., Harnack, Nygren, Bultmann) imposes a questionable scheme on history.

1.6   Modern Catholic thought has employed the category of development (see Newman) to avoid this pejorative interpretation of historical change. This development is an unfolding of what is implicit in the original event. Hence the New Testament or the Christ event remains the authority, but what it means only becomes apparent in the course of the life of the church. The scope of understanding grows. This view makes the actual course of the church's life the norm for determining the true meaning of the original event. It thus requires that later interpretations, such as Chalcedonian Christology, be read back into the original texts as their actual, even if only implicit, meaning and intention. This view thereby weakens the ability of the texts to encounter the later life and doctrine of the church as something foreign and normative over against it. And it unhistorically assimilates the experience and intention of the present church and that of primitive Christians.

II

2.1   In seeking a way beyond the recent state of New Testament scholarship, James M. Robinson calls for a more processive approach, which naturally arouses the interest and hope of a process theologian such as myself. This paper is intended to stimulate conversation between notions of process that emerge in biblical scholarship and those that derive from philosophical and theological considerations.

2.2   Many historians use the word "tradition" to refer to a historical process. Robinson hears this word as defining the continuity too much by the content of what is transmitted. The more important level of existential meaning is not brought into view in the usual story of the transmission of traditions. To allow for a fresh view of this more basic level of historical process, Robinson proposes a new term, "trajectory." The purpose of this paper is to comment on that image and Robinson's intentions in using it from the perspective of process thought. In general the criticism is of the image, which is that of a substantial entity moving through time with only external relations to the rest of the world. The assumption is that, far from being essential to Robinson's intention, the substantialist elements of the image are in conflict with his own sensitivity. The hope is that reflection based on a philosophy of events instead of substances will prove helpful to biblical scholars.

2.3   Current scholarship has broken up the unity of the New Testament materials and of the communities they reflect at theologically important levels. There are many messages which were regarded as Christian, and many of these found their way into the canon. Others can be discovered through the study of the canonical materials and other sources for the reconstruction of early Christianity. The multiplicity cannot be adequately treated in a single chronological sequence; for in each period alternative views of Christianity struggled for leadership. On the other hand, one cannot identify a set of views that survived intact through any extended period. But simply to recognize that multiplicity has the last word and to treat each formulation as an independent fact would be to abandon the full historical task with its normative element. What we need is to see how each formulation arose out of particular past ones in their interaction with new situations. One can see how a particular impetus gives rise to a new form as the situation changes.

III

3.1   Whitehead (cf. 56) identifies this kind of phenomenon as an historic route of occasions. Each occasion inherits from the past occasions in the route and transmits what it inherits to its successors. But each occasion is also affected by all the other occasions in its environment, and each introduces some element of its own creative response. This Whiteheadian idea fits well with what Robinson is saying. However, it introduces considerations that are not explicit in Robinson's presentation. Four are worth noting.

3.2   (1) The image of trajectories suggests that the several trajectories are so formed by the initiating impetus and the situational field that they can be described in mutual independence of one another as quite distinct and discrete entities. This is not Robinson's intention. Whitehead shows how the several historic routes influence one another by constituting part of the situational field for one another, and that their distinctness and discreteness is a matter of emphasis or degree. The basic situation is one of a vast multiplicity of events. Within that situation one can trace patterns of impressive order. In some cases the extent to which one event is shaped by a particular series of past events is so dominant that it may be considered as a member of that series and as relatively separable from other factors in its environment. But more commonly an event is shaped by multiple factors such that it can be viewed as a member of more than one historic route. The identification of clear-cut trajectories is then as much a matter of the questions historians ask as of the objective facts they investigate. But this does not make it unimportant.

3.3   (2) Robinson's image of trajectories also fails to highlight the elements of creative novelty in the events that make up the trajectory. Perhaps the fact that "trajectories" are usually of bits of matter discourages the needed emphasis on the decisional aspects of these events. It is too easy to think of the trajectory as determined exhaustively by the impetus of the past and the force of the field through which the entity passes. Robinson does not intend this materialistic view, but I think it is important to emphasize that the historic routes he traces are self-determining as well as externally caused.

3.4   (3) Normally in a trajectory the direct cause of the locus at any given point is found in the impetus transmitted by the preceding point on the trajectory together with the new field which has been entered. But normatively in most Christian trajectories a major factor in each period is reencountering of the originating events, that is, the reading of sacred texts, the proclamation of their meaning, and the reenactment of sacred rites. Hence, in addition to the originating impetus of those events, their conscious reconsideration is an important factor in forming the trajectory. This is better reflected in considering a series of occasions constituting an historic route, each of which takes account not only of immediate past members of the route but also, in memory, of more distant ones.

3.5   (4) A final advantage of the notion of an historic route over a trajectory is that it does not conjure up so strongly the image of a single all-decisive originative impetus. It allows for the recognition that several streams of events may have flowed together to constitute the route and that, however important a particular past event was as a distinctive impetus, it was itself part of an historic route and not its absolute beginning. This relativization does not, I think, run counter to Robinson's intentions.

IV

4.1   One of the most attractive features of Robinson's image of trajectory is that it turns us away from the question of a self-identical essence of Christianity. As I understand it, the unity of the trajectory is not found in a common essence or form at all points along the trajectory. That is, it is not necessary that we be able to state some common character exemplified in all the historical expressions which we identify as belonging to a given trajectory. Instead the unity of the trajectory is a causal continuity which allows for change. What happens at later points on the trajectory is deeply affected by what happens at earlier points, but it is not simply repetitive. There is no necessity that any specific feature of the early stages of the trajectory be repeated unchanged in later stages. We do not have to discover an identical belief, way of life, or mode of existence at all points on the trajectory in order to recognize its unity.

4.2   I am not sure how fully Robinson wants to accept this aspect of what I take to be the implication of his image. He seems reluctant to give up the idea of an essence of Christianity. But the image itself cuts against that way of thinking and so does much of his detailed analysis. Indeed, I am convinced that as historians describe what has occurred with greater and greater concreteness, diversities become more and more apparent, and the effort to trace identities through the shifting scene become more and more questionable. It is more fruitful to see how changes occurring in one event pave the way for new situations and new problems than to seek what is unchanging in the midst of this flux.

4.3   In this respect Whitehead's general discussion of historic routes is also inadequate. He understands historic routes to be identified by some common form transmitted from occasion to occasion. That form may be more or less important in the total constitution of the several occasions, but an occasion in which it is entirely absent is, by definition, not a member of that historic route.

4.4   To find help in Whitehead for the discussion of an identity not based on a common form, we must turn to his consideration of living occasions (cf. 102). He stresses that what is distinctive about life is novelty, and that living entities therefore do not ordinarily constitute historic routes in the sense described. But in persons a new kind of identity through time is attained. This identity is not achieved by the endless transmission of a particular form but by the canalization of originality: what emerges as a novel response in one living occasion is inherited by its successor, which is then free to add its own originative response (cf. Whitehead:107-8). In this way there can be growth, in which many of the novel achievements of the past become enduring elements in their successors. There can also be decay, in which more is lost in transmission than is added. Although Whitehead himself does not make this point, the identity of the living person is not a function of the intactness of any one of these forms. Indeed, each occasion creates its own synthesis of what it inherits, and in the process it modifies all the elements. Identity through time is maintained when successors include, transform, and build upon what they have received. Whitehead describes this as an "historic route of living occasions" (119), and we will call it a living historic route.

4.5   Since this point is of particular importance for the tracing of trajectories or of living historic routes, some further clarification is in order. When a community is not vital it can retain its identity as a community only by maintaining some identity of form. Repetition insures that the community is always the same. Many civilizations, once they have flowered, have then reenacted the forms attained and thus maintained their identity. There is no question but that trajectories or historic routes of this kind can be traced. But what is traced is necessarily in decay; for endless repetition is at the price of the intensity and zest that were originally present in what is repeated.

4.6   A vital community, on the other hand, is oriented more to the future than to the past. The past is more resource for new and creative response to opportunities and challenges than pattern to be reiterated or preserved. The identity of a living community is found, therefore, more in the form of its change than in its unchanged preservation of particular forms.

4.7   What we require are ways of discerning when change is the appropriate novel expression of a vital movement and when it is betrayal or decay. When is change a continuation of the trajectory and when is it a break from it? Whitehead's analysis of an "historic route of living occasions" gives us a clue to how the historian may consider this question. Formally, the answer can be stated as follows. Change is appropriate development or healthy growth when central elements in the historic route encourage the emergence of novel forms capable at once of enlivening much of the content of that route and of appropriating potential contributions from other sources. Change is betrayal when, for the sake of appropriating elements foreign to the historic route, the continuing contribution of that route is curtailed or blocked.

V

5.1   The interpretation of early Christianity as a multiplicity of partly independent interconnecting living historic routes paves the way for direct consideration of the normative question. Of these trajectories, which are responsibly Christian? Are they all Christian insofar as they intend to be so? Or are we to accept the judgement of history as to which are orthodox and which heretical? Or have we the possibility of making our own judgement, so that we are not limited to considering the actual outcome in the present church to be the final norm?

5.2   I am not clear as to Robinson's answer to these questions. They are difficult ones, and any answer must in some measure be circular. The criteria we employ for understanding what is "Christian" reflect the trajectories in which we stand. Still something can be said, and we can avoid turning our particular beliefs into norms for all times and places.

5.3   My approach is a relativistic one, but within this relativity I have strong judgements of what constitutes fuller faithfulness. I shall begin with minimal considerations and introduce others in what I take to be an ascending scale. That is, the higher criteria specify those events and movements which are more fully Christian.

5.41   First, historians and theologians need to differentiate Christianity from other human movements quite apart from any judgement of worth. In this sense the Crusades, the Inquisition, the persecution of witches, and the opposition to evolutionary theory are all parts of Christian history. It is generally agreed that movements stemming in a primary way from Jesus, his followers, and/or the New Testament are all part of Christianity. Of course, as considered this way, movements are more or less Christian according to the strength of these influences.

5.42   Second, a further dimension is added where there is the intention to be Christian. True, we may judge that what is done in the name of Christianity is benighted and perverse, but the intention to be Christian opens the way to its correction. Some acts done under the influence of Jesus but without the intent to be Christian are far more admirable in Christian eyes than many done consciously in the name of Christ. Nevertheless, the intention in itself renders the action more fully Christian.

5.43   Third, when the intention is informed by historical knowledge it is more fully Christian. That is, although historically uninformed action often intends to be appropriately faithful to Jesus or to the New Testament, it may be based on serious misjudgement. Action based on more accurate understanding is more likely to fulfill the intention of faithfulness. Hence, historical knowledge is a postitive contribution to being Christian. Such historical knowledge is itself many-layered. (a) It may mean only that the intention is checked against authoritative sources openly investigated. (b) It may mean also that there is an awareness of the historical difference between the sources and subsequent Christianity, and some consideration of the meaning of that difference. (c) It may mean that distinctions are recognized within the sources. (d) It may mean that one's own existence is understood in a fully historical way. (e) One may see Christianity in the context of the whole of history, including the other religions.

5.44   Fourth, whereas historical consciousness at a certain level is compatible with the view that to be Christian is to reenact some form from the past, it expresses itself most fully when it frees one from this kind of faithfulness. Thus one is more fully Christian when one's inheritance from the Christian past enables one to be open to the future instead of needing to repeat the past.

5.45   Fifth, openness to the future is completed through openness to traditions other than Christianity. To be most completely faithful to Christianity is to be conscious of fulfilling one's faithfulness in the fullest possible appropriation of whatever appears as true and valuable wherever it is to be found. This does not entail wholesale acceptance of other traditions. Instead it requires original, critical, and creative incorporation of their contributions. Such incorporation contributes to the life of a movement, whereas rejection of new wisdom involves defensiveness, repetition of the old forms without the spirit they originally expressed, and inevitable decay.

5.5   These normative criteria for Christianity are continuous with descriptive ones. Where there is the serious intention to be Christian, one tends to try to understand Christianity historically. Where historical understanding is achieved, one tends to be freed from the view that faithfulness consists in reenactment of past forms. Where one is freed from that view, one experiences Christian faith as opening one to all truth and as encouraging original, critical, and creative responses. Of course people who travel that route often continue to define Christianity in terms of past forms that restrict, so that what I am calling ideally Christian is closely related to what many regard as post-Christian or even anti-Christian. From my perspective those who reject Christianity while moving in this trajectory are still Christian in the sense of the first criterion, but they are in danger of ultimately undercutting their own achievements by losing the intention to be Christian.

VI

6.1   In evaluating trajectories in early Christianity, these criteria presumably would have some relevance. Among trajectories intending to be Christian all to some extent assimilated the historical events to mythical meanings; but while some lost the historical grounding of faith in this process, others refused to obscure their historical basis. Among those that held fast to the historical character of their faith and paid attention to the actual meanings of their traditions, all sought conformation of present patterns to the forms of originating events to some extent; but while some became slavishly bound to past forms, others responded more freely to new challenges. Among those which were relatively free to respond to new situations creatively, all excluded much that was valuable and true in traditions other than their own; but while some were rigidly narrow, others were remarkably able to appropriate selectively and imaginatively from non-Jewish religion, philosophy, and law.

6.2   All the early Christian historic routes continue in some measure pre-Christian historic routes, most of which are Jewish. The continuity is mediated through Jesus and/or through the believing response to him. The Old Testament is our major source for understanding the earlier phases of these historic routes. Like all important events in a living historic route, the events surrounding Jesus introduced important discontinuities into these routes so that the Christian forms of these routes differ from the Jewish forms. In the discontinuity much of value and importance was added, but as with all such discontinuities, much of value and importance was also lost and has been better preserved and developed in historic routes that remained Jewish. Some of this can be regained in subsequent interaction with these closely related routes as well as through the repeated reappropriation of elements in the common ancestry of both sets of living routes.

6.3   From our present perspective within living historic Christian routes, we can discern that much of the impetus we now experience is derived from events in primitive Christianity, from Jesus, and from the earlier Jewish tradition. We do not need, however, to discover our norms explicitly in our sources. The impetus to freedom may have in its original context restrictions that in later phases of the route are rejected and overcome. Thus what freedom means to a contemporary Christian may be quite different from what it meant for Paul, and it would not matter if the difference were greater still or if different words were used to express it. It would remain true that Paul's talk of freedom, both as a link in the route and as an idea to be wrestled with again and again, has given important impetus through the whole subsequent route.

6.4   If these formal and abstract comments about trajectories and living historic routes are to be more than that, actual historical works must embody them. It is my hope that the time is at hand when the potential fruitfulness for historical study of this philosophy of events can be concretely tested.

WORKS CONSULTED

Bultmann, R.
1951–55   *Theology of the New Testament.* 2 vols. Trans. K. Grobel. New York: Scribners.

Ebeling, G.
1966   *Theology and Proclamation: Dialogue with Bultmann.* Trans. J. Riches. Philadelphia: Fortress.

Harnack, A.
1961   *History of Dogma.* 7 vols. Trans. N. Buchanan. New York: Dover.

Newman, J. H.
1905   *An Essay in the Development of Christian Doctrine.* London: Toovey.

Nygren, A.
1969   *Agape and Eros: A Study of the Christian Idea of Love.* Trans. P. S. Watson. New York: Harper and Row.

Robinson, J. M.
1971   "Introduction: The Dismantling and Reassembling of the Categories of New Testament Scholarship." Pp. 1–19 in *Trajectories through Early Christianity.* With H. Koester. Philadelphia: Fortress.

Whitehead, A. N.
1978   *Process and Reality: An Essay in Cosmology.* Corrected Edition. Eds. D. R. Griffin and D. W. Sherburne. New York: Free Press/Macmillan. Original, 1929.

COBB'S LIVING HISTORIC ROUTES:
A RESPONSE

Kent Harold Richards
The Iliff School of Theology

ABSTRACT

Although John Cobb's view is based on a philosophy of events, the current hermeneutical discussion focuses on literature and language. Nevertheless, Cobb has made a contribution to the discussion of the indeterminacy of meaning. Viewed from the process perspective of his concept of a "living historic route," interpretation is an imaginative act. Lev 27:1-8, for example, when interpreted from this perspective, can evoke a sense of the sanctification of persons without the repetition of a common form of sexist and ageist valuation.

0.1   The stated purpose of Cobb's paper is to comment on the image and intention of Robinson's term trajectory. The term was devised as a way to move beyond the static, substantialist implications of the word tradition. Since the publication of Robinson's essay and since the first draft of Cobb's paper (1975) was shared with the Process Hermeneutic and Biblical Exegesis Group of the Society of Biblical Literature the term, trajectory, has become a part of the *dictionary* of biblical studies. Course titles have utilized the term as well as articles and monographs. There has been little serious reflection, so that Cobb's criticism that the term is still "that of a substantial entity moving through time with only external relations to the rest of the world" persists. He raises the possibility that some additional reflections based on a philosophy of events might lead toward new biblical and historical conclusions.

0.2   Robinson in a 1975 oral response stated that he had no "great pride of invention or any particular reason to defend" the term's adequacy. He noted that there had been little discussion among Germans since the German edition "slouched back into German idealism's technical term for development" when translating trajectory. He went on to say, "I think that the kinds of criticism of the symbolism that John makes in his paper were in part the same motivations I had in reaching for this term."

    This leaves the focus of my comments not on the term but the implications suggested by Cobb. He says that it should be determined whether or not "a philosophy of events instead of substances will prove helpful to biblical scholars."

0.3   A response must be selective since a multitude of hermeneutical issues are raised. Let me comment in three ways. First, a restatement of the issue as I find it portrayed in Cobb's paper. Second, a formal and abstract response to the proposal. Third, a brief application of Lev 27:1–8.

1.   First, a restatement of the issue

1.1   I come to Cobb's paper not as a process theologian and may miss some of the essential and foundational implications. I am grateful that the technical Whiteheadian vocabulary is held to a minimum because that in itself can be a barrier to any dialogue. Despite the lack of technical terminology the paper is saturated with Whiteheadian presuppositions. Cobb has provided a bridge from more traditional biblical jargon to his alternative terminology, living historic route. This transition is a minimal requirement for any new theory.

1.2   Cobb's philosophy of events encourages him to suggest that historical study is important beyond being able to demonstrate that it is a mere heuristic tool, guide to the present, prognosticator of the future, or illustration of the multiplicity and futility of human understanding. He believes that biblical studies have all too frequently taken one of these stances.

1.3   He proposes that Whitehead's understanding of an historic route of occasions and his reflections on an identity not based on a common form (living occasions) will provide an alternative to both the concept tradition and Robinson's term trajectory. The alternative image, living historic route, presents a way to emphasize the multiplicity of factors in any event or series of events. An event can participate in more than one route. An event is both continuous and discontinuous with its situational field. The novelty of the event(s) contributing to any living historic route can be identified more readily since it is separable and not only identifiable through continuity and/or end results. Furthermore, the separability of events constituting a living historic route permits both originative events and reencountered events to shape the route. The historian must take into account not only chronologically successive events but the entire situational field which is made up of discrete yet interdependent events. The identification of the living historic route is not through a common form. This implies that a living historic route is found more in an identity of change than in one of repetition.

1.4   These concepts lead Cobb to the specific task of Christian theology. He states that Christianity is "a multiplicity of partly independent interconnecting living historic routes." This understanding liberates the past from contemporary Christianity determining "the true meaning of the original event." On the other hand, it ties the past to the present in that the inheritance is a potential source of novelty. These understandings should encourage the biblical scholar to seek with renewed vigor a reencounter with the text since that constitutes a formative event in living historic routes.

2. A formal and abstract response

2.1 First, the effort to bring theologian and biblical scholar into dialogue is laudable. Biblical theology of almost every variety works from a perspective which denies the applicability of imposed systematic categories. Theologians are no doubt heartened by the biblical scholars who are admitting the necessity of better understanding their own philosophical, phenomenological and linguistic presuppositions.

The current hermeneutical discussion among many biblical scholars has turned from the problems associated with history and historiography to a focus upon literature and criticism. This to some extent signals a move away from the Cobb-Robinson concerns. The "eye of the storm" in much of the current discussion is found in deconstruction which debates issues of literal and figurative meanings of words, the freedom of a piece of literature from author, and what some have called a hermeneutics of indeterminacy. Despite this shift it would be naive to assume that the questions of history have no place in the literary conversation. Cobb has not directly engaged this debate. The living historic route does presuppose that the literature we have arises from authors within identifiable (albeit problematic) events. Cobb does not make suggestions regarding the distinctiveness of the written text and the possibilities of using Whitehead's understanding of language. Nevertheless, we have access to the living historic route both as it constitutes itself in the present and as it is encountered/reencountered in the text's memory of more distant events. Others working in this arena have made proposals regarding Whitehead's theory of language and the implications for an understanding of text.

2.2 This leads to the second comment. Some biblical scholars will be ecstatic to find a theologian interested in the text's "ability" to influence the contemporary theological task. Cobb is concerned that the Christian theologian not "unhistorically assimilate" the past with the present. The contention is that when a philosophy of events is developed the biblical scholar can, and indeed must, contribute to the identification of what it means to be faithful to a present living historic route.

The living historic route focuses not on the transmission of some essence or common form but on the canalization of originality. In the past when the biblical scholar traced identity in time, "what is traced is necessarily in decay; for endless repetition is at the price of the intensity and zest that were originally present in what is repeated." Of course, there is a recognition that change does not automatically constitute faithfulness to the living historic route. Therefore, the criteria of faithfulness must always be considered from within the interdependent events of the route so that the "actual outcome in the present" will not contain the ultimate criterion. A measure of circularity and relativization is present but not at the risk of a permanent suspension of decision-making.

These suggestions, while clearly bringing the biblical scholar into the arena of contemporary meaning, will raise questions about the necessary distancing traditionally expected from any hermeneutic. The historical-literary critical method's contribution has resided in allowing the biblical scholar distance from the text. Thereby a text could genuinely present us with something novel. Cobb's living historic route intends to give distance through the recognition that an originative event as witnessed in the biblical text can be recovered over against the present. For the present is constituted not only of the traces of decaying and novel living historic routes but also contributes its trace. The biblical scholar must be willing to acknowledge that normativity also arises outside the biblical text.

2.3   This last observation leads to the "eye of the storm" within Cobb's paper. The biblical scholar can laud the theologian who suggests dialogue, can give thanks that biblical and historical study will make a difference, but turn off further discussion when there is any acknowledgment that the interpreter's participation is anything but distant, let alone normative in reading a text. It seems to me that Cobb is able through the image of living historic routes to allow a text its own space as well as acknowledge the space of the interpreter.

The living historic route permits an acknowledgment of the multiplicity of events. These events are both self determining and externally determining. They are generated by originative impetus, successive events and the reencountering of those events.

As I turn to a biblical text I need not discover some identity over time which fits the past with the present. I can examine what factors occasioned the text, discuss how those factors relate to diverse living historic routes, and determine what successive occasions, including the present, inherit, synthesize and modify. The interpretive task from a process perspective does not end with a description or a suspension of judgment but in an imaginative act which evokes both living on the edge and determining where the edge exists.

3.   A brief application of Lev 27:1–8

3.1   . . . your valuation of a male from twenty years old up to sixty years old shall be fifty shekels. . . . If the person is a female, your valuation shall be thirty shekels. If the person is from five years old up to twenty years old, your valuation shall be for a male twenty shekels, and for a female ten shekels. If the person is from a month old up to five years old, your valuation shall be for a male five shekels . . . and for a female . . . three shekels. . . . And if the person is sixty years old and upward, then your valuation for a male shall be fifteen shekels, and for a female ten shekels. And if the man is too poor to pay your valuation, then . . . the priest shall value him; according to the ability of him who vowed. . . .

Lev 27:1-8 (RSV)

Reported here within a speech of the Lord to Moses is the valuation of individuals according to age and sex. [Without getting into the traditio-historical questions of the text, let me suggest that] in this appendix to the Holiness Code there are suggested monetary equivalences for persons dedicated to the Lord. These monetary equivalences fulfill the vow of a person and hence the release of that person from the vow. Since in later times there were Levitical functionaries within the cult, these dedicated persons were no longer needed and a monetary equivalence was worked out. This meant that personal commitments in a changed social situation were commuted to monetary commitments. This type of commutation is not unique to the dedication of persons but is found elsewhere in Israel's traditions.

For the moment what is intriguing is that you have the valuation of persons according to sex and seasons of life. My eleven and fifteen year old daughters are worth ten shekels; Michael, the neighbor boy who is ten, is worth twice as much—twenty shekels. My mother who is over sixty is worth ten shekels—the same as my daughters. My wife is worth thirty shekels and I am worth fifty shekels. Of course, if one is poor they can hope that the priest will take seriously the provision to allow the payment according to the ability to pay.

One implication seems clear—males between twenty and sixty years of age are of the greatest worth! Apart from this implication, which at the beginning of the 80's may be enough to incite a riot, there are at least several intriguing points which need to be mentioned. First, the commutation for females five to twenty years of age is identical to females over sixty. The implications of this are many. As it were, the middle years have value over either end of the chronology. Youth must *not* have been the valued quantity. A second intriguing point is that the male over sixty is worth less than the male under twenty (twenty shekels as compared to fifteen). Here youth would seem to be predominant in value. A third point is the interesting fact that when the male reaches beyond sixty years of age the valuation drops thirty-five shekels, while the female over sixty drops only twenty shekels in value. An implication would seem to be that a more dramatic decline would need to be integrated in the male's self-understanding as opposed to the female's. A final point needs to be drawn; namely, that the valuations are not entirely absolute, since in the case of the poor the priest can set the payment. The implications here for ecclesiastical politics are infinite!

3.2   This is the way I began a paper for a conference on aging. I had been asked what the Bible might contribute to a theology of aging. This led me to look for the biblical traditions on the subject. There were texts which might have come to anyone, such as Eccl 12:1-7, which focuses the complexity and seriousness of Israel's attention to the seasons of life.

Remember also your Creator in the days of your youth, before the evil days come, and the years draw nigh, when you will say, "I have no pleasure in them"; before the sun and the light and the moon and the stars are darkened and the clouds return after the rain; in the day when the keepers of the house tremble, and the strong men are bent, and the grinders cease because they are few, and those that look through the windows are dimmed, and the doors on the street are shut; when the sound of the grinding is low, and one rises up at the voice of a bird, and all the daughters of song are brought low; they are afraid also of what is high, and terrors are in the way; the almond tree blossoms, the grasshopper drags itself along and desire fails; because man goes to his eternal home, and the mourners go about the streets; before the silver cord is snapped, or the golden bowl is broken, or the pitcher is broken at the fountain, or the wheel broken at the cistern, and the dust returns to the earth as it was, and the spirit returns to God who gave it.

Eccl 12:1-7 (*RSV*)

In addition, one could turn to the interesting word-field designating individuals at various stages of life. Texts like Jer 6:11 and 51:22 distinguish nearly a dozen Hebrew terms that imply three-, four- or five-part classifications according to age. Furthermore, another set of texts could point to the characteristics of various seasons of life. The old man in Psalm 71 demonstrates the fear of loneliness, loss of importance in community and reduced physical strength. The young woman is characterized by beauty as expressed throughout the Song of Solomon. The young men, while many times not wanting to take responsibility, do have strength and are important to family and nation (Gen 42:35-38; Prov 20:29).

3.3   This gives some impression of how one might begin to work with the text. Also, it leads back to the beginning of Cobb's paper—the role of historical study. I could construct a so-called biblical tradition which would identify the characteristics of the text's understanding of the seasons of life. However, the disparate events out of which the tradition would be constructed might be more likely to trace the successive events out of which the texts evolved so that the end result would be the essence of aging.

If I attempted to look to implications I could use the Leviticus passage to point up the text's view of male superiority. I could demonstrate the sensitivity of the text to the poor in that they were to pay based on ability. Or, I could take an entirely different posture and leave my work at a descriptive point with ample documentation regarding the considerable disunity of Israel's traditions. I would never need to comment on implications since my task as a biblical scholar would rest upon description. There are, of course, other alternatives but I do not think that these are unfair characterizations of how we biblical scholars have worked.

3.40   I can turn now to the image of living historic routes sharing some of the contours of this context. Let me address three issues which I think can illustrate the merits of Cobb's proposal.

3.41   First, the living historic route conceptuality allows the interpreter to preserve the contrast between the events surrounding the text and the interpreter's world. I was intrigued by the valuations of human beings and indicated some of those factors. However, the context surrounding Leviticus 27 is one of sanctification involving the movement of objects, space, time and persons from being profane to being holy. The chapter deals with the gifts offered. The intersection of the text's sanctification issue and my interests with the valuation need not be dissolved. In fact, that meeting brings new questions to the text just as the text's concerns press for a novel inclusion of sacred and profane factors in the valuation of humans.

3.42   Second, the insistence that the living historic route is found more in the identity of change than the repetition of a common form leads to some formative factors. Within Judaism there is a remarkable repetition of the common form found in Leviticus 27. I mention only once instance, namely *Arakhin*, which deals in six of its eight chapters with Lev 27:1-8. One can demonstrate beyond any doubt the reenactment of the forms from Leviticus but the more remarkable factor is the novelty which emerges. Neusner has taken an important step in illustrating this when he deals with this document.

If one turns to Christianity one finds no continuing route like that of Judaism. However, if one were to pursue such a text in Irenaeus, the route of sanctification would be reencountered. The text (*Against Heresies* 2.22.4; Roberts/Donaldson:391) says of Jesus:

> ... He also possessed the age of a Master, not despising or evading any condition of humanity, nor setting aside in Himself that law which He had appointed for the human race, but sanctifying every age, by that period corresponding to it which belonged to Himself. For He came to save all through means of Himself—all, I say, who through Him are born again to God—infants, and children, and boys, and youths, and old men. He therefore passed through every age, becoming an infant for infants, thus sanctifying infants; a child for children, thus sanctifying those who are of this age, being at the same time made to them an example of piety, righteousness, and submission; a youth for youths, becoming an example to youths, and thus sanctifying them for the Lord. So likewise He was an old man for old men, that He might be a perfect Master for all, not merely as respects the setting forth of the truth, but also as regards age, sanctifying at the same time the aged also, and becoming an example to them likewise. Then, at last, He came on to death itself, that He might be "the first-born from the dead, that in all things He might have the pre-eminence," the Prince of life, existing before all, and going before all.

3.43   Finally, the contemporary reencountering of the Leviticus text can make its own contribution. Despite the severe contrast between a context of sanctification and my concern for the valuation of human beings there rests the notion of commutation. Some have suggested that the very practice of dedicating and vowing a person to the sanctuary was a commuting of the sacrifice of a human life on the altar. One might say that behind the dedication of a person to the sanctuary lies human sacrifice, just as behind the monetary valuation of persons lies the dedication of a person to the sanctuary. In other words, the Leviticus text is at least a second level of commutation.

It is necessary, when reading the Leviticus text from the perspective of a philosophy of events, that one pay attention to the routes between Moses and the Levitical priests, between the world of human sacrifice and dedicated human beings, and between the sacred and the profane. Once this larger perspective is reached it is obligatory to look deep within the text and the interpreter. Therein will rest a "vision of ourselves as dancers in an endless space, finite dancers in a space not infinite but undefined" (Snodgrass).

WORKS CONSULTED

Neusner, Jacob
1979 *A History of the Mishnaic Law of Holy Things.* Studies in Judaism in Late Antiquity, 30/4. Leiden: E. J. Brill.

Richards, Kent Harold
1978 "Shekels and the Seasons of Life." An unpublished paper read 1 May 1978 at a Conference on Aging in Denver, Colorado.

Roberts, A. and Donaldson, J. (eds.)
1925 *The Ante-Nicene Fathers.* American reprint of the Edinburgh edition. Revised and arranged, with prefaces and notes by A. C. Coxe. Vol. 1. New York: Scribners.

Snodgrass, S. D.
1975 *In Radical Pursuit.* New York: Harper & Row.

PROCESS HERMENEUTIC: PROMISE AND PROBLEMS

John J. Collins
DePaul University

ABSTRACT

Biblical theology should be both public and critical. Process theology offers a public philosophical basis beyond confessional faith. Some questions arise as to its critical character. An initial problem concerns the Process notion of God. If God is the "principle of concretion" it is not clear in what sense he is an "actual entity" or why this principle should be called God rather than nature. A second problem concerns the nature and status of biblical language. Can we assume that this language contains reliable metaphysical information or should it rather be read as expressive of human emotions and conceptions? Further questions are whether, and in what sense, biblical portrayals of, e.g., obedience can now be considered normative, and how does Process theology deal with elements in the biblical text (e.g. divine coercion) which are not congenial to its perspective?

0. Preliminary observations

0.1 The importance of presuppositions has been repeatedly emphasized in modern hermeneutics and the point is especially obvious in biblical theology. It may fairly be said that the much trumpeted crisis in biblical theology has arisen in large part from the welter of unexamined and often concealed presuppositions. It may be well, then, to state at the outset what I look for in biblical theology and so clarify the perspective from which I evaluate the Process approach.

0.2 My first requirement of biblical theology is that it be public—i.e. that it rest on warrants and premises which are accessible for examination by any reasonable human being (Tracy:1981a, b). A theological proposal which insists on a particular formulation of Christian faith as a precondition for dialogue is inaccessible to anyone who doesn't share that particular confessional stance. Many biblical theologies are inadequate for this reason, not only the conservative fundamentalist ones but also the currently fashionable canonical approach of B. S. Childs. Faith may well be the goal of biblical theology, but it cannot be the starting point unless the circle of conversation is limited to a closed group of believers, in isolation from society at large.

0.3   Second, biblical theology should be critical. The biblical text should not be accepted unquestioningly in any sense. Biblical scholars are often warned against the historical naïveté of assuming that the texts should be read as history. This is only one dimension of the problem. We should equally beware of moral naïveté, of assuming that conduct which is recorded with apparent approval is therefore virtuous (Genesis 22 is a notorious test case). We must also avoid the metaphysical naïveté of assuming that biblical statements about God (or about human nature, for that matter) are *necessarily* either true or meaningful. Just as the historicity of biblical narratives can only be evaluated in the light of our other sources and historical analogies, so the moral and metaphysical claims must be assessed in the light of our knowledge of reality from all sources. Before a biblical assertion can be evaluated we must know the evidence on which it is based, or which can be adduced to support it. Even more fundamentally, we must know the kind of assertion we are dealing with. It makes a world of difference whether Genesis 2–3 should be read as a scientific account of the origin of the world (in admittedly metaphorical dress) or as a fictional representation of the universal human condition. A critical reading of the Bible requires an appreciation of the varieties of biblical language and the genres of biblical literature.

0.4   Process theology rests on explicit philosophical foundations, which are available for public discussion, provided, of course, that the pronouncements of Whitehead are not given dogmatic status. I find no problem in the foregoing articles in that regard. The attempt to relate biblical theology to a credible contemporary scientific and philosophical view of the world is admirable and must be especially welcomed in the face of the current drift to confessionalism. The critical character of the undertaking is more complex and requires some reflection. I will address what I see as the two main issues raised in these essays, the nature of God and the normative character of the biblical text, and use the passages which have been adduced from Hosea 11, Numbers 22–24 and Leviticus 27 to focus the discussion.

1.   The nature of God

1.1   Theology is by definition talk about God, and so the understanding of God plays a cardinal role in any theological proposal. The nature of God is at issue in all the discussion here, but is most directly addressed in the essay of Gerald Janzen.

1.11   Janzen undertakes "to hunt for passages which might be adduced in support of a process versus a classical view of God." His thesis is that "a process view of things may dispense with many traditional hermeneutical devices designed to 'save the [biblical] appearances,' since it provides a current thought and language within which we may interpret *along* the metaphorical grain, and not *against* the grain, those Old Testament portrayals where God's passionality and mutability are either asserted or assumed" (Janzen:§3.0).

1.12   Now it seems to me to be beyond doubt that the God of the OT, and conspicuously of Hosea, is a God who changes and who is affected by human actions. The indeterminacy of the divine aim, which Mays finds problematic, seems to me to be compatible with much of the OT, although it would have to be modified somewhat in the case of the apocalyptic literature. However, a happy coincidence with Process theology in these matters is not in itself an adequate warrant for a Process hermeneutic. The adequacy of the Process account of reality must first be judged on its own merits. If biblical theology is to be credible and meaningful in the contemporary world, then the basic issue is not whether it is compatible with Process theology, but whether Process thought is itself coherent and persuasive. Any modern philosophical system will inevitably introduce categories which are quite alien to the OT, but by so doing it can enable us to relate the Bible to modern views of reality. Whether or not one has to interpret the Bible against the grain would scarcely be an issue if we were convinced that classical theism provides a better account of reality by philosophical and scientific standards.

1.13   I should say at the outset that I have no stake in defending the immutable passionless God of classical theology. That view of God cannot now be defended on philosophical or scientific grounds, and receives no support from the Bible either. The issue is not classical theism versus Process theism, but whether it is possible to give any coherent and persuasive philosophical account of God at all. The corollary of this problem in biblical exegesis is whether a passage like Hosea 11 should at all be presumed to give metaphysical information or should rather be read as an expression of human sentiments and emotions.

1.14   The coherence and persuasiveness of Process theism have been argued by Whitehead, Hartshorne and others. It would be unreasonable to expect a full presentation in every discussion of Process hermeneutics. Cobb, Janzen and Ford have all provided helpful summaries elsewhere (Cobb and Griffin:1976; Janzen:1976; Ford:1978). An adequate critique of Process theism is also far beyond the scope of this response and my own philosophical competence. All I can do here is indicate an area which remains for me problematic. The Process God is "the principle of concretion" imminent in the world, who (a) "orders pure possibilities so that they are available in grades of relevance vis-à-vis the actual world" and (b) "supplies the initial aim for each emergent actual entity" (Janzen, 1976:494). God can be described as a "lure" towards "intensity of harmonious feeling," which does not coerce but exercises a persuasive attraction. Yet this God is regarded as an "actual entity" (which is "an occasion of experience, a 'throb of experience'" [Janzen, 1976:486]). God can "be conceived either as a principle or as a person. Conceived as a principle, God really is very much like Plato's Form of the Good, that is, the principle of order or value in terms of which all the possibilities are organized. Alternatively, one could conceive of God as a personal being who 'thinks on thinking,' to use the Aristotelian phrase" (Ford, 1978:9–10).

1.15   It should be apparent that the personal conception of God is "mythical" or metaphorical, and is optional rather than necessary. Indeed, Whitehead affirmed that "the deeper truths must be adumbrated by myths" (Janzen, 1976:493) and ultimately any portrayal of a personal God must be recognized as metaphorical. What remains unclear to me, however, is why, or how, a God who is the "principle of concretion" should be conceived as an "actual entity" rather than as a factor, tendency or principle, in actual entities. It is not apparent to me why this principle should be called "God" rather than, say, "nature." I wonder whether Whitehead's notion of God is not guilty of his own "fallacy of misplaced concreteness."

1.2   The nature of prophetic language

1.21   My first problem, then, is with the coherence of the Process notion of God in itself. It is in any case apparent that the "mutability and passionality" of the "Principle of concretion" have vast philosophical implications which are scarcely hinted at in the book of Hosea. Even in the context of a Process hermeneutic, those who cry "metaphor" and "anthropomorphism" (Janzen:§3.0) are quite right. A process of de-mythologizing is implied here, just as surely as in existentialist hermeneutic, even if we are reminded that the poetic language of myth is ultimately able to give a fuller and more satisfactory account of reality (Janzen, 1976:493). The question, as Janzen rightly notes, is not *whether* we should attempt to de-mythologize, but *how* we should do so, and this will depend on our judgment on the kind of language we are dealing with. Janzen reads Hosea 11 as informative language, admittedly in a metaphorical mode/1/. Hosea's metaphors are taken to refer to the reality of God as understood by Process theology. So the divine self-questioning in Hos 11:8–9 describes the process of concretion by which conflicting factors are harmonized in a new wholeness. It is, of course, quite evident that Hosea did not arrive at this description by philosophical analysis. If it matches the philosophical description in significant respects, this must be credited to the prophet's intuition of reality (perhaps "blessed of God" in Ford's phrase) or be regarded as coincidence.

1.22   The outcome of Hos 11:8–9 is that "the transformed divine aim ensures that Yahweh will not turn to destroy Ephraim." In fact, we know that Ephraim was destroyed. Presumably, the divine aim had to be revised in the light of subsequent developments since "God's aims must continually be adapted to the limitations of particular occasions" (Coats:§8.1). Since the Process God does not exercise full control over the world in any case (Ford, 1978:20) the divine aim does not ensure anything absolutely. In this perspective God is limited by the world and mankind and so the contrast between God and humankind in Hos 11:9 becomes less emphatic. But how does one assess the reality of a divine aim which does not come to fulfillment? What reason is there to believe that Hos 11:9 gives information about a divine intention when the actual course of events came out so differently?

1.23   One might of course argue that Hos 11:9 is a reliable report of a divine intention because it conforms to "*yiḥud*" or the tendency towards harmonious feeling which is characteristic of the God of Process theology. However, this character is not always so obvious in the God of Hosea. In 13:14 another existential question is answered in a manner no less decisive than chap. 11: "O Death, where are your plagues? O Sheol, where is your destruction? Compassion is hid from my eyes." The passage goes on to prophesy that "Samaria shall bear her guilt . . . their little ones shall be dashed in pieces, and their pregnant women ripped open." It is obvious enough that this passage corresponds to historical reality, but not so obvious that it "perfectly exemplifies the true character of *yiḥud*, of existential decision toward holistic becoming" (Janzen:§6.2). One could argue, I suppose, that the divine aim was adapting to the limitations of a new occasion, but this smacks of special pleading. There is no real evidence that Israel's religious performance or the general political situation changed so radically within the time span when these oracles were delivered/2/.

1.3   An alternative approach

1.31   There are of course other ways of reading Hosea. Since the oracles are so blatantly anthropomorphic there is good reason to believe that they were developed by analogy with human behavior. We may then reasonably suspect that the prophet is projecting his own emotions onto God, or that his language is *expressive*, of his own emotions, rather than *informative*, about God. The existential questions, then, are primarily human dilemmas—the familiar human experience of being torn between two impulses. One impulse prevails in chap. 11, the other in chap. 13. (I find Janzen's interpretation of *yaḥad* forced, and find Mays's response persuasive on this point). Hos 11:9 functions, then, as a model for human decisions: it is better to be compassionate than to destroy.

1.32   This text stands out as one of the great "break-through" texts of the OT by its affirmation of values in human relations. To be sure, this lofty sentiment is not maintained. The fluctuation between compassion and destructiveness may have been caused to some degree by a changing situation, where destruction was more obviously imminent at some times than at others. More fundamentally, it seems to me, the differences are due to two different functions which God-language serves throughout the Bible. On the one hand, whatever happens is ascribed to God ("If it is not he, who then is it?" Job 9:24). On the other hand God-language serves to express human ideals. What God does ought to be good, and our understanding of what is good can only be derived from human experience. These two functions of God-language do not always coincide. In the case of Hosea, the harsh reality of Assyrian power indicated that compassion was hid from Yahweh's eyes. On the other hand, the prophet's sense of values insisted that compassion was better than destructive force. Hosea was neither the first nor the last to learn that the God of moral idealism is not always the God of historical reality.

1.33   It seems to me that such a social-historical approach adequately accounts for the oracles of Hosea as human statements. Such an approach frees us from the necessity of positing unfulfilled divine intentions. Moreover, as a general hermeneutical principle, it leaves room for the possibility that some biblical statements may be ideological expressions without metaphysical value. Even if we are disposed to agree that Hos 11:8-9 is a revelatory statement, since it expresses sentiments which are worthy of God, the fact remains that the verse describes human emotions which are then applied to God by analogy. We affirm that one who is God and not man ought to be compassionate, because we know the value of compassion from human experience. Accordingly, it seems to me that an interpretation of Hosea's oracles as language expressive of human sentiments rests on a sounder basis than one which posits a coincidence between prophetic intuition and Process metaphysics.

2.   Normative status

2.1   The question of prophetic language touches already on the second major issue raised in this volume, the normative status of the Bible. I can heartily endorse George Coats's critique of B. S. Childs's insistence on the canonical form. The discordant voices within the biblical tradition cannot be so easily dismissed. The discussion of what blessing might mean in a Process perspective, by both Coats and Ford, is highly interesting. Yet two problems remain.

2.11   The first concerns the adequacy of a Process framework for biblical hermeneutics. If the legend of Balaam as saint can be interpreted in terms of divine persuasion, but the fable of Balaam as sinner involves coercion, does this mean that the categories of Process thought are only partially applicable to the Bible? How does Process theology deal with passages which imply divine coercion? Must these be interpreted "against the grain," in Janzen's phrase? These questions bear on the nature and status of biblical language. Is the whole Bible, or only part of it, assumed to be informative about the metaphysical realities which we otherwise know through Process thought?

2.12   My second question concerns the normative character of Balaam's obedience, and indeed of the whole tradition which links blessing with obedience. Blessing here is understood "not as a reward for obedience previously given" but as "the character and form of the life of obedience itself" (Coats:§§6.61–6.62). Virtue is its own reward. Of course, not all obedience is virtuous. It is assumed here that the virtue lies in obedience to God, which is by definition acceptance of the good. The question, then, concerns again the status of biblical narratives. Can we assume that whatever the Bible presents as obedience to God is really such?

2.2   An alternative approach

2.21   When I read the Balaam story in Numbers 22-24 I am most impressed by their propagandistic character. The focal point of the story is surely the emphatic insistence that God has blessed Israel. The four oracles of blessing dominate the story by their length and repetition. While the narrative may be compatible with divine persuasion, the emphasis does not fall on the freedom of Balaam's response. Quite the contrary: "How can I curse whom God has not cursed?" "He has blessed and I cannot revoke it." At no point does one get the impression that Balaam has a real option in the matter. He is bound by the prior decision of God. Even in the fable in Numbers 22, Balaam's sin is a matter of ignorance. Once he sees the angel of the Lord, there is no question of disobedience. The fable shows the futility, even impossibility for Balaam of resisting the will of God. While I agree with Coats that the fable derives from a different tradition, the juxtaposition with the legend here casts a shadow over the presumed freedom of Balaam's response.

2.22   The final emphasis of the story falls on the blessing of Israel, not of Balaam. Balaam may be logically included in the formula "blessed be everyone who blesses you," but the specific blessing of Balaam is implicit, not explicit, and the story says nothing about its fulfillment. Accordingly, I cannot agree that the story belongs in the same field of tradition as Genesis 22, or Job. Rather the Balaam story seems to me to be a propagandistic glorification of Israel. We know that the figure of Balaam was known outside of biblical tradition. Numbers 22-24 shows two ways in which Israel could deal with the reputation of a famous pagan seer. One way is to adopt him, and assert that he really obeyed the God of Israel and affirmed the blessing of Israel. This attitude towards famous pagan authorities becomes widespread in the Hellenistic age and early Christianity. Balaam here is the forerunner of the Sibyl. The second way is to expose the famous seer to ridicule, which is done rather delightfully in the fable of Numbers 22. This attitude to pagan religion is more typical of the Hebrew Bible. We might compare the story of Elijah mocking the prophets of Baal on Mt. Carmel (1 Kings 18) or Second Isaiah's ridicule of Babylonian idols. The unifying factor in the fable and the legend is the ultimate glorification of Israel and its God. This interpretation fits well with Sanders's description of the canonical process (Coats:§4.5). A tradition must be adaptable to different literary forms and to the varying fortunes of people who found their identity in it. Numbers 22–24 preserves two adaptations of the Balaam tradition, each of which could serve to bolster Israelite identity in face of the renown of a pagan seer.

2.23   Obviously there is much more to be said about Numbers 22–24. I only wish here to indicate the lines along which a social-historical interpretation would proceed. One of my main misgivings about the Process hermeneutic is that it fails to reckon with ideological factors in the biblical text. It seems to me that no contemporary hermeneutic can ignore such questions without appearing naïve. I should hasten to add that Process hermeneutic is neither the only nor the worst offender in this regard.

2.3   Historic routes

2.31   Similar questions arise in connection with the Process revision of the notion of tradition. Cobb's explanation of "historic routes" is admirable and does indeed provide a better and more nuanced understanding of what we usually call tradition or trajectory. I suspect that I am like many biblical scholars if I nonetheless hesitate to adopt the new terminology, since it may carry more philosophical implications than are readily apparent to me. The technical terminology of a philosophy should probably not be accepted piece-meal, but in the context of its full system. I also think that such terms as tradition and trajectory remain serviceable, although Cobb's discussion can help us nuance our understanding.

2.32   My question here is how far this understanding of historic routes helps us address normative questions. Kent Richards has helpfully provided a test-case (Leviticus 27) to focus the discussion. I agree that it is helpful to be aware of the different historic routes: of the different facets of the text (sanctification as well as valuation), subsequent adaptions of the tradition and the correlation with contemporary values. Yet I would like to hear more of what Richards sees when he "looks deep within the text and the interpreter" (Richards:§3.43). It is not clear to me that we have really advanced beyond the descriptive point, with documentaton of the disunity of the tradition.

2.33   My own approach to the contemporary appropriation of a passage like Leviticus 27 is to regard it as input with which Christian life should be informed (cf. Gustafson:1970) but I cannot regard it as normative in any sense that demands assent or obedience. The text might be used in various ways. One might, like Richards, emphasize the notion of commutation, and take the text as a precedent for commuting biblical or traditional stipulations which are out-dated or seen to be deficient. One might equally well see in it the danger of establishing a hierarchy of sanctification, the dehumanizing effect of subordinating people to the demands of cultic symbolism. A biblical text such as this can inform us negatively as well as positively. Fidelity to the tradition is not in itself the primary requirement of the moral life, unless the tradition itself is viewed as the quest for the human good. It may be that my approach here is substantially in agreement with Cobb's view of Christian faith "as opening one to all truth and encouraging original, critical, and creative responses" (Cobb:§5.5).

3. Conclusion

3.1   It is my assumption in this response that the authors of these essays seek to commend Process hermeneutic as a framework for biblical study. I welcome the undertaking, as a refreshing affirmation of the public character of theology, at a time when there is a widespread drift to confessionalism. I have sought, however, to indicate some of the reasons why I am not yet persuaded to adopt this approach. I would like to see a clearer exposition of the Process notion of God. Here more effort will have to be made to translate the technical terminology of Whitehead, if Process thought is to be made accessible to the majority of biblical scholars. I would also like to see some clearer statements on the status of the Bible. The question whether this is a revelatory book which can be assumed to give reliable metaphysical information, or is rather an expression of human conceptions and aspirations of variable value, is one which cannot ultimately be avoided. Finally, it seems to me that Process theology will have to go beyond the search for quasi-proof texts which show a surface similarity to Process theism. If Process hermeneutic is to prove adequate it must deal equally with those aspects of the tradition which are not congenial to its categories.

3.2   In all, I feel that a good deal of ground must be traversed before Process hermeneutic can provide the dominant categories for biblical study. Yet the dialogue is a stimulating one. If it promotes reflection on the philosophical presuppositions of biblical study, it can only prove beneficial.

NOTES

/1/   For the distinction of "informative," "expressive" and other kinds of language, see Caird (7–36).

/2/   Wolff (197) dates chap. 11, very tentatively, to the period 727–724 and chap. 13 "very probably" around 724 (224).

WORKS CONSULTED

Caird, G. B.
1980   *The Language and Imagery of the Bible.* Philadelphia: Westminster.

Cobb, John B., Jr. and Griffin, David R.
1976   *Process Theology: An Introductory Exposition.* Philadelphia: Westminster.

Ford, Lewis S.
1978   *The Lure of God: A Biblical Background for Process Theism.* Philadelphia: Fortress.

Gustafson, James
1970   "The Place of Scripture in Christian Ethics: A Methodological Study." *Int* 24:430–55.

Janzen, J. Gerald
1976   "The Old Testament in 'Process' Perspective: Proposal for a Way Forward in Biblical Theology." Pp. 480–509 in *Magnalia Dei: The Mighty Acts of God. Essays on the Bible and Archeology in Memory of G. Ernest Wright.* Eds. F. M. Cross, W. E. Lemke and P. D. Miller. New York: Doubleday.

Tracy, David
1981a   "Defending the Public Character of Theology." *The Christian Century* 98:350–56.

1981b   *The Analogical Imagination: Christian Theology and the Culture of Pluralism.* New York: Crossroad.

Wolff, Hans Walter
1974   *Hosea: A Commentary on the Book of the Prophet Hosea.* Hermeneia. Trans. G. Stansell. Philadelphia: Fortress.

www.ingramcontent.com/pod-product-compliance
Lightning Source LLC
Chambersburg PA
CBHW032302150426
43195CB00008BA/544